Disclaimer

Book Title: NIST Cloud Computing Standards Roadmap

Book Author: Annie W. Sokol; Michael D. Hogan

Book Abstract: NIST has been designated by the Federal Chief Information Officer (CIO) to accelerate the federal government's secure adoption of cloud computing by leading efforts to develop standards and guidelines in close consultation and collaboration with standards bodies, the private sector, and other stakeholders. Standards are critical to ensure cost-effective and easy migration, to ensure that mission-critical requirements can be met, and to reduce the risk that sizable investments may become prematurely technologically obsolete. Standards are key elements required to ensure a level playing field in the global marketplace. The NIST Cloud Computing Standards Roadmap Working Group has surveyed the existing standards landscape for interoperability, performance, portability, security, and accessibility standards/models/studies/use cases/conformity assessment programs, etc., relevant to cloud computing. Using this available information, current standards, standards gaps, and standardization priorities are identified within this document.

Citation: NIST SP - 500-291r2

Keyword: Cloud computing; standards; roadmap

NIST Cloud Computing Standards Roadmap

NIST Cloud Computing Standards Roadmap Working Group
NIST Cloud Computing Program
Information Technology Laboratory

NIST **National Institute of Standards and Technology** • U.S. Department of Commerce

This page left intentionally blank

NIST Special Publication 500-291,
Version 2
(Supersedes Version 1.0, July 2011)

NIST Cloud Computing Standards Roadmap

NIST Cloud Computing Standards

Roadmap Working Group

July 2013

U. S. Department of Commerce
Penny Pritzker, Secretary

National Institute of Standards and Technology
Patrick D. Gallagher, Under Secretary of Commerce for Standards and Technology and Director

This page left intentionally blank

Reports on Computer Systems Technology

The Information Technology Laboratory (ITL) at the National Institute of Standards and Technology (NIST) promotes the U.S. economy and public welfare by providing technical leadership for the nation's measurement and standards infrastructure. ITL develops tests, test methods, reference data, proof of concept implementations, and technical analysis to advance the development and productive use of information technology. ITL's responsibilities include the development of technical, physical, administrative, and management standards and guidelines for the cost-effective security and privacy of sensitive unclassified information in federal computer systems. This document reports on ITL's research, guidance, and outreach efforts in Information Technology and its collaborative activities with industry, government, and academic organizations.

National Institute of Standards and Technology Special Publication 500-291 V2

Natl. Inst. Stand. Technol. Spec. Publ. 500-291, 108 pages (May 24, 2013)

DISCLAIMER

This document has been prepared by the National Institute of Standards and Technology (NIST) and describes standards research in support of the NIST Cloud Computing Program.

Certain commercial entities, equipment, or material may be identified in this document in order to describe a concept adequately. Such identification is not intended to imply recommendation or endorsement by the National Institute of Standards and Technology, nor is it intended to imply that these entities, materials, or equipment are necessarily the best available for the purpose.

Acknowledgements

This document is an update of the first version, which was published in July 2011. It reflects the contributions and discussions by the membership of the NIST Cloud Computing Standards Roadmap Working Group, chaired by Michael Hogan and Annie Sokol of the Information Technology Laboratory, National Institute of Standards and Technology, U.S. Department of Commerce.

NIST SP 500-291, Version 2 has been collaboratively authored by the NIST Cloud Computing Standards Roadmap Working Group. As of the date of this publication, there are over one thousand Working Group participants from industry, academia, and government. Federal agency participants include NASA and the U.S. Departments of Agriculture, Commerce, Defense, Health & Human Services, Homeland Security, Justice, Transportation, Treasury, State, and Veterans Affairs.

NIST would like to acknowledge the specific contributions from the following Working Group members:

Alan Sill, Open Grid Forum
Annie Sokol, NIST
Craig Lee, Open Grid Forum
David Harper, Johns Hopkins University
Eugene Luster, U.S. Department of Defense
Frederic de Vaulx, NIST
Gary Massaferro, AlloyCloud, Inc.
Gilbert Pilz, Oracle Corporation
Jerry Smith, US Department of Defense
John Calhoon, Microsoft
John Messina, NIST
Michael Hogan, NIST
Michael Stewart, Space and Naval Warfare Systems Command
Michaela Iorga, NIST
Nancy Landreville, University of Maryland
P W Carey, Compliance Partners, LLC
Paul Lipton, CA Technologies
Richard Brackney, Microsoft
Robert Bohn, NIST
Robert Marcus, Cloud Standards Customer Council
Shin Adachi, NTT Multimedia Communications Labs
Steven McGee, SAW Concepts LLC
Steven Woodward, Woodward Systems
Sundararajan Ramanathan, Capgemini US Consulting
Winston Bumpus, DMTF, VMWare Inc.

The NIST editors for this document were: Michael Hogan and Annie Sokol.

TABLE OF CONTENTS

LIST OF FIGURES

LIST OF TABLES

Foreword

This is the second edition of the NIST Cloud Computing Standards Roadmap, which has been developed by the members of the public NIST Cloud Computing Standards Roadmap Working Group. This edition includes updates to the information on portability, interoperability, and security standards in the first edition and adds new information on accessibility and performance standards. Also new in this edition is information on the role of conformity assessment in support of voluntary consensus standards. Analyzing typical government use cases (see Section 8), U.S. Government priorities and gaps in cloud computing voluntary consensus standards are identified in this edition and the previous edition. This information is intended for use by federal agencies and other stakeholders to help plan their participation in voluntary consensus standards development and related conformity assessment activities, which can help to accelerate the agencies' secure adoption of cloud computing.

1 EXECUTIVE SUMMARY

The National Institute of Standards and Technology (NIST) has been designated by the Federal Chief Information Officer (CIO) to accelerate the federal government's secure adoption of cloud computing by leading efforts to identify existing standards and guidelines. Where standards are needed, NIST works closely with U.S. industry, standards developers, other government agencies, and leaders in the global standards community to develop standards that will support secure cloud computing.

Consistent with NIST's mission,[1] the NIST Cloud Computing Program has developed a *USG Cloud Computing Technology Roadmap*, as one of many mechanisms in support of United States Government (USG) secure and effective adoption of the Cloud Computing model [2] to reduce costs and improve services. Standards are critical to ensure cost-effective and easy migration, to ensure that mission-critical requirements can be met, and to reduce the risk that sizable investments may become prematurely technologically obsolete. Standards are key elements required to ensure a level playing field in the global marketplace, [3] The importance of setting standards in close relation with private sector involvement is highlighted in a memorandum from the White House: M-12-08,[4] dated January 17, 2012.

The NIST Cloud Computing Standards Roadmap Working Group has surveyed the existing standards landscape for interoperability, performance, portability, security, and accessibility standards/models/studies/use cases/conformity assessment programs, etc., relevant to cloud computing. Where possible, new and emerging standardization work has also been tracked and surveyed. Using this available information, current standards, standards gaps, and standardization priorities are identified within this document.

---

[1] This effort is consistent with the NIST role per the National Technology Transfer and Advancement Act (NTTAA) of 1995, which became law in March 1996.

[2] *NIST Definition of Cloud Computing*, Special Publication 800-145, "Cloud computing is a model for enabling ubiquitous, convenient, on-demand network access to a shared pool of configurable computing resources (e.g., networks, servers, storage, applications, and services) that can be rapidly provisioned and released with minimal management effort or service provider interaction."

[3] This edition of the standards roadmap focuses on USG cloud computing requirements for interoperability, performance, portability, security, and accessibility, and does not preclude the needs to address other essential requirements.

[4] *Principles for Federal Engagement in Standards Activities to Address National Priorities*, January 17, 2012 http://www.whitehouse.gov/sites/default/files/omb/memoranda/2012/m-12-08.pdf

The NIST Definition of Cloud Computing identified cloud computing as a model for enabling ubiquitous, convenient, on-demand network access to a shared pool of configurable computing resources (e.g., networks, servers, storage, applications, and services) that can be rapidly provisioned and released with minimal management effort or service provider interaction.

As an extension to the above NIST cloud computing definition, a NIST cloud computing reference architecture has been developed by the NIST Cloud Computing Reference Architecture and Taxonomy Working Group that depicts a generic high-level conceptual model for discussing the requirements, structures and operations of cloud computing. It contains a set of views and descriptions that are the basis for discussing the characteristics, uses, and standards for cloud computing, and relates to a companion cloud computing taxonomy.[5]

Cloud computing use cases describe the consumer requirements when using cloud computing service offerings. Through its working groups as described below, the NIST Cloud Computing program has studied a range of U.S. federal government and general-purpose use cases to extract features that are amenable to standardization. Using these examples, the current document analyzes how existing cloud-related standards fit the needs of federal cloud consumers and identifies standardization gaps.

Cloud computing standards are already available in support of many of the functions and requirements. While many of these standards were developed in support of pre-cloud computing technologies, such as those designed for web services and the Internet, they also support the functions and requirements of cloud computing. Other standards have been developed or are now being developed to support specific cloud computing functions and requirements, such as virtualization, infrastructure management, service level agreements (SLAs), audits and cloud-specific data handling. Wherever possible, applicable standards are identified in this document.

To assess the state of standardization in support of cloud computing, the NIST Cloud Computing Standards Roadmap Working Group has compiled an Inventory of Standards Relevant to Cloud Computing.[6] This inventory is being maintained and updated as necessary. Using the taxonomy developed by the NIST Cloud Computing Reference Architecture and Taxonomy Working Group, cloud computing relevant standards have been mapped to the requirements of accessibility, interoperability, performance, portability, and security.

---

5 NIST Special Publication 500-292, *NIST Cloud Computing Reference Architecture*, September 2011 http://www.nist.gov/customcf/get_pdf.cfm?pub_id=909505

6 http://collaborate.nist.gov/twiki-cloud-computing/bin/view/CloudComputing/StandardsInventory

Present areas with standardization gaps include: SaaS (Software as a Service) functional interfaces; SaaS self-service management interfaces; PaaS (Platform as a Service) functional interfaces; business support / provisioning / configuration; security; and privacy. Present standardization areas of priority to the federal government include: security auditing and compliance; identity and access management; SaaS application specific data and metadata; and resource description and discovery.

While there are only a few approved cloud computing specific standards at present, there is a fast-changing landscape of cloud computing-relevant standardization under way in a number of Standards Developing Organizations (SDOs). Every effort has been made in the context of the NIST Cloud Computing Standards Roadmap to engage with and to gather input from SDOs active in this area. Federal agencies should also be encouraged to participate specifically in cloud computing standards development projects that support the specific needs and priorities of their cloud computing services. Specific recommendations regarding engagement between federal agencies and SDOs are:

Recommendation 1 – Contribute Agency Requirements

Agencies should coordinate and contribute clear and comprehensive user requirements for cloud computing standards projects.

Recommendation 2 – Participate in Standards Development

Agencies should actively participate and coordinate in cloud computing standards development projects that are of high priority to their agency missions. The January 17, 2012, White House Memorandum, M-12-08, [7] lists five fundamental strategic objectives for federal government agencies whenever engaging in standards development.

Recommendation 3 – Encourage Testing to Accelerate Technically Sound Standards-Based Deployments

Agencies should support the concurrent development of conformity and interoperability assessment schemes to accelerate the development and use of technically sound cloud computing standards and standards-based products, processes, and services. Agencies should also include consideration of conformity assessment approaches currently in place that take account of elements from international systems, to minimize duplicative testing and encourage private sector support.

[7] Principles for Federal Engagement in Standards Activities to Address National Priorities, January 17, 2012

Recommendation 4 – Specify Cloud Computing Standards

Agencies should specify cloud computing standards in their procurements and grant guidance when multiple vendors offer standards-based implementations and there is evidence of successful interoperability testing.

Recommendation 5 – USG-Wide Use of Cloud Computing Standards

To support USG requirements for accessibility, interoperability, performance, portability, and security in cloud computing, the Federal Cloud Computing Standards and Technology Working Group, in coordination with the Federal CIO Council Cloud Computing Executive Steering Committee (CCESC) and the Cloud First Task Force, should recommend specific cloud computing standards and best practices for USG-wide use.

2 INTRODUCTION

2.1 BACKGROUND

U.S. laws and associated policy require federal agencies to use international, voluntary consensus standards in their procurement and regulatory activities, except where inconsistent with law or otherwise impractical.

The National Institute of Standards and Technology (NIST) has been designated by the Federal Chief Information Officer (CIO) to accelerate the federal government's secure adoption of cloud computing by leading efforts to identify existing standards and guidelines. Where standards are needed, NIST works closely with U.S. industry, standards developers, other government agencies, and leaders in the global standards community to develop standards that will support secure cloud computing.

The NIST Cloud Computing Program was formally launched in November 2010 and was created to support the federal government effort to incorporate cloud computing as a replacement for, or enhancement to, traditional information system and application models where appropriate.

The NIST Cloud Computing Program operates in coordination with other federal cloud computing implementation efforts (CIO Council/Information Security and Identity Management Committee [ISIMC], etc.) and is integrated with the Federal CIO's 25-point IT Implementation Plan for the federal government.

At the beginning of 2011, NIST created the following public working groups in order to provide a technically oriented strategy and standards-based guidance for the federal cloud computing implementation effort:

- Cloud Computing Reference Architecture and Taxonomy Working Group
- Cloud Computing Standards Acceleration to Jumpstart Adoption of Cloud Computing (SAJACC) Working Group
- Cloud Computing Security Working Group
- Cloud Computing Standards Roadmap Working Group
- Cloud Computing Target Business Use Cases Working Group

2.2 NIST CLOUD COMPUTING VISION

NIST seeks to provide leadership and guidance around the cloud computing paradigm to catalyze its use within industry and government. NIST also strives to shorten the adoption life cycle, which will enable near-term cost savings and increased ability to quickly create and deploy safe and secure enterprise solutions. Furthermore, NIST is committed to foster cloud computing practices that support interoperability, portability, and security requirements that are appropriate and achievable for various usage scenarios, by focusing on the necessary standards, specifications, and guidance that must be in place for these requirements to be met.[8]

The NIST area of focus is technology, and specifically, interoperability, portability, and security requirements, standards, and guidance. In this version of the document, accessibility and performance have also been included. The intent is to use the standards strategy to prioritize NIST tactical projects which support USG agencies in the secure and effective adoption of the cloud computing model to support their missions. The expectation is that these priorities will benefit industry, SDOs, cloud adopters, and policy makers.

In this document, privacy as a standards issue is narrowly dealt with under confidentiality, a subset of information security. Confidentiality includes preserving authorized restrictions on access and disclosure, including means for protecting personal privacy. Because privacy requirements are mostly policy decisions, they are often developed by governments as laws and not by SDOs. Appendix J of NIST Special Publication 800-53, Revision 4, *Security and Privacy Controls for Federal Information Systems and Organizations*, includes a catalog of privacy controls for federal information systems and organizations and a process for selecting controls to protect organizational operations, organizational assets, individuals, other organizations, etc., from a diverse set of threats including hostile cyber-attacks, natural disasters, structural failures, and human errors (both intentional and unintentional).

[8] SP 500-293 Volume II, US Government Cloud Computing Technology Roadmap Volume II (Draft) Release 1.0 http://www.nist.gov/itl/cloud/upload/SP_500_293_volumeII.pdf

2.3 NIST CLOUD COMPUTING STANDARDS ROADMAP WORKING GROUP

SDOs and others have and are developing supporting cloud computing documents to include standards, conceptual models, reference architectures, conformity assessment programs, and standards roadmaps to facilitate communication, data exchange, and security for cloud computing and its application. Still other standards are emerging to focus on technologies that support cloud computing, such as virtualization. The NIST Cloud Computing Standards Roadmap Working Group is leveraging this existing, publicly available work, plus the work of the other NIST working groups, to develop a NIST Cloud Computing Standards Roadmap that can be incorporated into the NIST USG Cloud Computing Technology Roadmap.

2.4 HOW THIS REPORT WAS PRODUCED

The NIST Cloud Computing Standards Roadmap Working Group (CCSRWG) has surveyed the existing standards landscape for interoperability, performance, portability, security, and accessibility standards / models / studies / use cases / conformity assessment programs, etc., relevant to cloud computing. Using this available information, standards, standards gaps or overlaps, and standardization priorities have been identified, thereby providing a clearer picture of this evolving technical landscape.

3 THE NIST DEFINITION OF CLOUD COMPUTING [9]

Cloud computing is a model for enabling ubiquitous, convenient, on-demand network access to a shared pool of configurable computing resources (e.g., networks, servers, storage, applications, and services) that can be rapidly provisioned and released with minimal management effort or service provider interaction. This cloud model is composed of five essential characteristics, three service models, and four deployment models.

Essential Characteristics:

On-demand self-service. A consumer can unilaterally provision computing capabilities, such as server time and network storage, as needed automatically without requiring human interaction with each service provider.

Broad network access. Capabilities are available over the network and accessed through standard mechanisms that promote use by heterogeneous thin or thick client platforms (e.g., mobile phones, tablets, laptops, and workstations).

Resource pooling. The provider's computing resources are pooled to serve multiple consumers using a multi-tenant model, with different physical and virtual resources dynamically assigned and reassigned according to consumer demand. There is a sense of location independence in that the customer generally has no control or knowledge over the exact location of the provided resources but may be able to specify location at a higher level of abstraction (e.g., country, state, or datacenter). Examples of resources include storage, processing, memory, and network bandwidth.

Rapid elasticity. Capabilities can be elastically provisioned and released, in some cases automatically, to scale rapidly outward and inward commensurate with demand. To the consumer, the capabilities available for provisioning often appear to be unlimited and can be appropriated in any quantity at any time.

Measured service. Cloud systems automatically control and optimize resource use by leveraging a metering capability [10] at some level of abstraction appropriate to the type of service (e.g., storage, processing, bandwidth, active user accounts). Resource usage can be monitored, controlled, audited, and reported, providing transparency for both the provider and consumer of the utilized service.

---

[9] NIST Special Publication 800-145, *NIST Definition of Cloud Computing*, September 2011

[10] Typically this is done on a pay-per-use or charge-per-use basis.

Service Models:

Software as a Service (SaaS). The capability provided to the consumer is to use the provider's applications running on a cloud infrastructure.[11] The applications are accessible from various client devices through either a thin client interface, such as a web browser (e.g., web-based email) or a program interface. The consumer does not manage or control the underlying cloud infrastructure including network, servers, operating systems, storage, or even individual application capabilities, with the possible exception of limited user-specific application configuration settings.

Platform as a Service (PaaS). The capability provided to the consumer is to deploy onto the cloud infrastructure consumer-created or acquired applications created using programming languages, libraries, services, and tools supported by the provider.[12] The consumer does not manage or control the underlying cloud infrastructure including network, servers, operating systems, or storage, but has control over the deployed applications and possibly configuration settings for the application-hosting environment.

Infrastructure as a Service (IaaS). The capability provided to the consumer is to provision processing, storage, networks, and other fundamental computing resources where the consumer is able to deploy and run arbitrary software, which can include operating systems and applications. The consumer does not manage or control the underlying cloud infrastructure but has control over operating systems, storage, and deployed applications, and possibly limited control of select networking components (e.g., host firewalls).

Deployment Models:

Private cloud. The cloud infrastructure is provisioned for exclusive use by a single organization comprising multiple consumers (e.g., business units). It may be owned, managed, and operated by the organization, a third party, or some combination of them, and it may exist on or off premises.

---

[11] A cloud infrastructure is the collection of hardware and software that enables the five essential characteristics of cloud computing. The cloud infrastructure can be viewed as containing both a physical layer and an abstraction layer. The physical layer consists of the hardware resources that are necessary to support the cloud services being provided, and typically includes server, storage and network components. The abstraction layer consists of the software deployed across the physical layer, which manifests the essential cloud characteristics. Conceptually the abstraction layer sits above the physical layer.

[12] This capability does not necessarily preclude the use of compatible programming languages, libraries, services, and tools from other sources.

Community cloud. The cloud infrastructure is provisioned for exclusive use by a specific community of consumers from organizations that have shared concerns (e.g., mission, security requirements, policy, and compliance considerations). It may be owned, managed, and operated by one or more of the organizations in the community, a third party, or some combination of them, and it may exist on or off premises.

Public cloud. The cloud infrastructure is provisioned for open use by the general public. It may be owned, managed, and operated by a business, academic, or government organization, or some combination of them. It exists on the premises of the cloud provider.

Hybrid cloud. The cloud infrastructure is a composition of two or more distinct cloud infrastructures (private, community, or public) that remain unique entities, but are bound together by standardized or proprietary technology that enables data and application portability (e.g., cloud bursting for load balancing between clouds).

4 CLOUD COMPUTING REFERENCE ARCHITECTURE

The NIST cloud computing definition is widely accepted and valuable in providing a clear understanding of cloud computing technologies and cloud services. The NIST cloud computing reference architecture presented in this section is a natural extension to the NIST cloud computing definition.

The NIST cloud computing reference architecture is a generic high-level conceptual model that is a powerful tool for discussing the requirements, structures, and operations of cloud computing. The model is not tied to any specific vendor products, services, or reference implementation, nor does it define prescriptive solutions that inhibit innovation. It defines a set of actors, activities, and functions that can be used in the process of developing cloud computing architectures, and relates to a companion cloud computing taxonomy. It contains a set of views and descriptions that are the basis for discussing the characteristics, uses, and standards for cloud computing.

The NIST cloud computing reference architecture focuses on the requirements of what cloud service provides, not on a design that defines a solution and its implementation. It is intended to facilitate the understanding of the operational intricacies in cloud computing. The reference architecture does not represent the system architecture of a specific cloud computing system; instead, it is a tool for describing, discussing, and developing the system-specific architecture using a common framework of reference.

The design of the NIST cloud computing reference architecture serves the objectives to: illustrate and understand various cloud services in the context of an overall cloud computing conceptual model; provide technical references to USG agencies and other consumers to understand, discuss, categorize, and compare cloud services; and communicate and analyze security, interoperability, and portability candidate standards and reference implementations.

4.1 OVERVIEW

The Overview of the Reference Architecture describes five major actors with their roles and responsibilities using the newly developing Cloud Computing Taxonomy. The NIST cloud computing reference architecture defines five major actors: cloud consumer, cloud provider, cloud auditor, cloud broker, and cloud carrier (See Figure 1: Cloud Actors). These core individuals have key roles in the realm of cloud computing. Each actor is an entity (a person or an organization) that participates in a transaction or process and/or performs tasks in cloud computing. For example, a Cloud Consumer is an individual or organization that acquires and uses cloud products and services. The purveyor of products and services is the Cloud Provider. Because of the possible service

[13] NIST Special Publication 500-292, *NIST Cloud Computing Reference Architecture*, September 2011

offerings (Software, Platform or Infrastructure) allowed for by the cloud provider, there will be a shift in the level of responsibilities for some aspects of the scope of control, security and configuration. The Cloud Broker acts as the intermediary between consumer and provider and will help consumers through the complexity of cloud service offerings and may also create value-added cloud services. The Cloud Auditor provides a valuable inherent function for the government by conducting the independent performance and security monitoring of cloud services. The Cloud Carrier is the organization which has the responsibility of transferring the data, somewhat akin to the power distributor for the electric grid.

Figure 1 – **Cloud Actors** briefly lists the five major actors defined in the NIST cloud computing reference architecture.

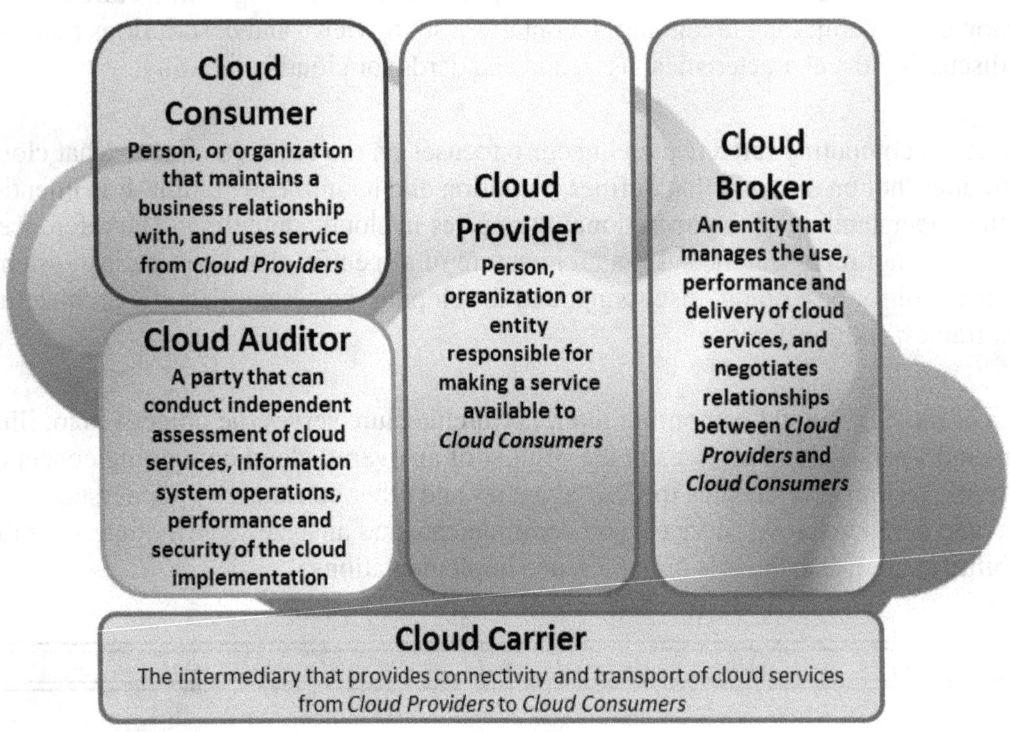

Figure 1 – Cloud Actors

Figure 2 – Interactions between the Actors in Cloud Computing shows the interactions among the actors in the NIST cloud computing reference architecture. A cloud consumer may request cloud services from a cloud provider directly or via a cloud broker. A cloud auditor conducts independent audits and may contact the others to collect necessary information. The details will be discussed in the following sections and be presented as successive diagrams in increasing levels of detail.

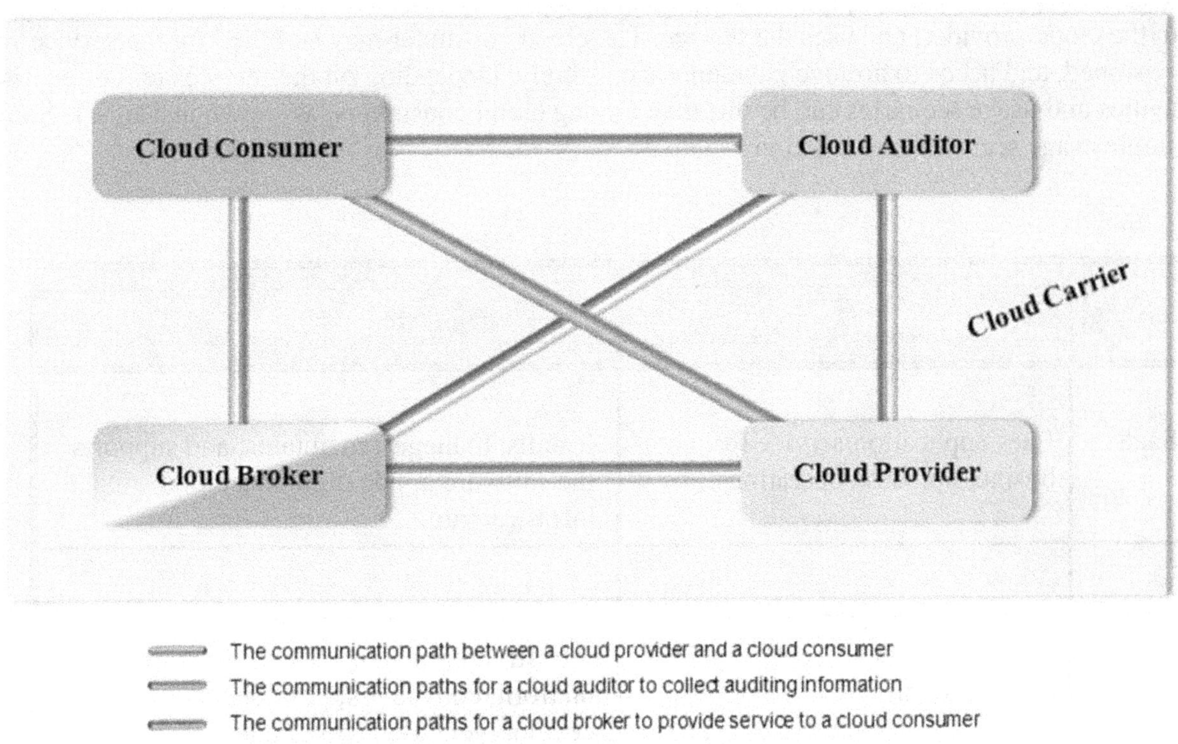

The communication path between a cloud provider and a cloud consumer
The communication paths for a cloud auditor to collect auditing information
The communication paths for a cloud broker to provide service to a cloud consumer

Figure 2 – Interactions between the Actors in Cloud Computing

4.2 CLOUD CONSUMER

The cloud consumer is the ultimate stakeholder that the cloud computing service is created to support. A cloud consumer represents a person or organization that maintains a business relationship with, and uses the service from, a cloud provider. A cloud consumer browses the service catalog from a cloud provider, requests the appropriate service, sets up service contracts with the cloud provider, and uses the service. The cloud consumer may be billed for the service provisioned, and needs to arrange payments accordingly. Depending on the services requested, the activities and usage scenarios can be different among cloud consumers, as shown in Table 1. Some example usage scenarios are listed in Figure 3.

Service Models	Consumer Activities	Provider Activities
SaaS	Uses application/service for business process operations.	Installs, manages, maintains, and supports the software application on a cloud infrastructure.
PaaS	Develops, tests, deploys, and manages applications hosted in a cloud system.	Provisions and manages cloud infrastructure and middleware for the platform consumers; provides development, deployment, and administration tools to platform consumers.
IaaS	Creates/installs, manages, and monitors services for IT infrastructure operations.	Provisions and manages the physical processing, storage, networking, and the hosting environment and cloud infrastructure for IaaS consumers.

Table 1 – Cloud Consumer and Cloud Provider

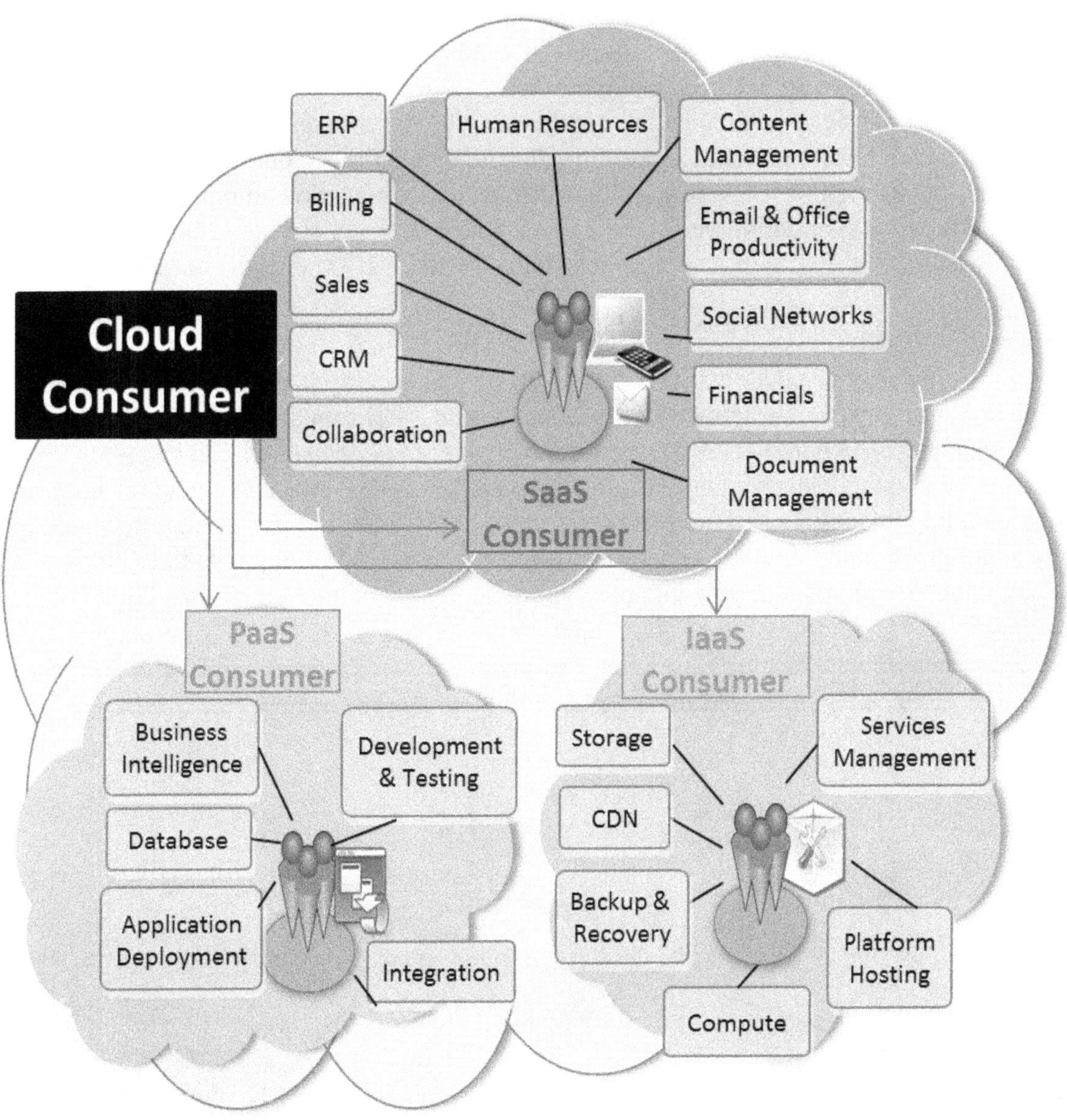

Figure 3 – Example of Services Available to a Cloud Consumer

SaaS applications are usually deployed as hosted services and are accessed via a network connecting SaaS consumers and providers. The SaaS consumers can be organizations that provide their members with access to software applications, end users who directly use software applications, or software application administrators who configure applications for end users. SaaS consumers access and use applications on demand, and can be billed on the number of consumers or the amount of consumed services. The latter can be measured in terms of the time in use, the network bandwidth consumed, or the amount/duration of data stored.

For PaaS, cloud consumers employ the tools and execution resources provided by cloud providers for the purpose of developing, testing, deploying, and managing applications hosted in a cloud system. PaaS consumers can be application developers who design and implement application software, application testers who run and test applications in various cloud systems, application deployers who publish applications into a cloud system, and application administrators who configure and monitor application performance on a platform. PaaS consumers can be billed by the number of consumers, the type of resources consumed by the platform, or the duration of platform usage.

For IaaS, consumers are provisioned with the capabilities to access virtual computers, network-accessible storage, network infrastructure components, and other fundamental computing resources, on which consumers can deploy and run arbitrary software. IaaS consumers can be system developers, system administrators, and information technology (IT) managers who are interested in creating, installing, managing and monitoring services for IT infrastructure operations. IaaS consumers are provisioned with the capabilities to access these computing resources, and are billed for the amount of resources consumed.

4.3 CLOUD PROVIDER

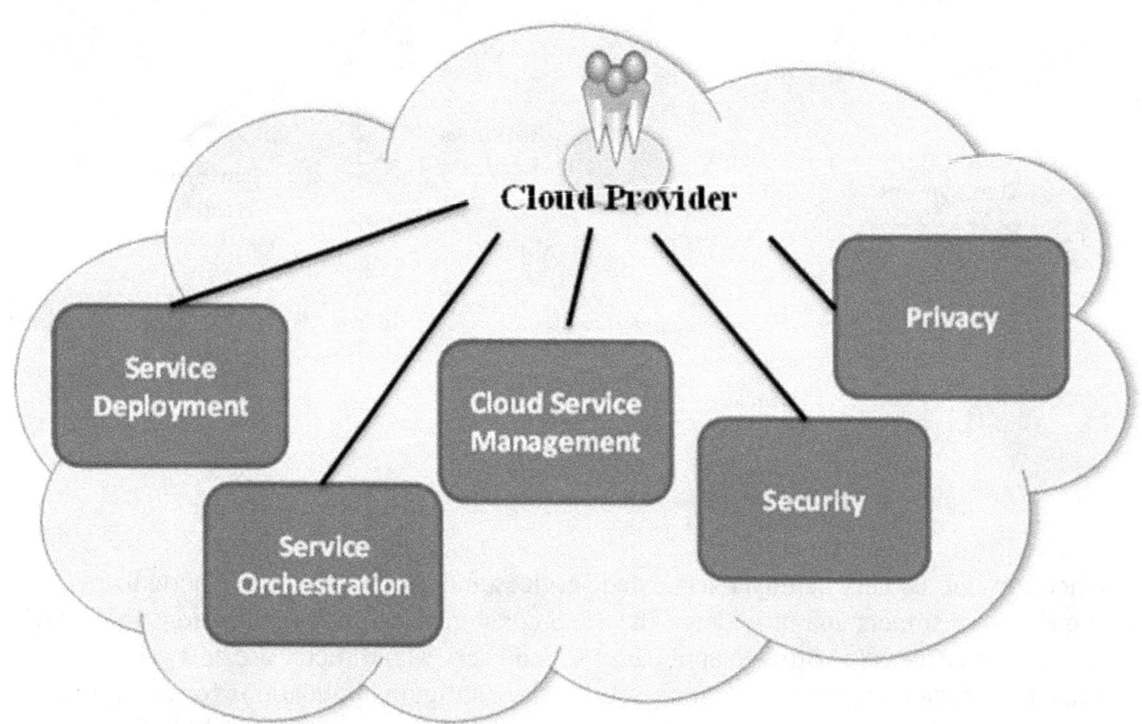

Figure 4 – Cloud Provider: Major Activities

A cloud provider can be a person, an organization, or an entity responsible for making a service available to cloud consumers. A cloud provider builds the requested software/platform/ infrastructure services, manages the technical infrastructure required for providing the services, provisions the services at agreed-upon service levels, and protects the security and privacy of the services. As illustrated in Figure 4 – Cloud Provider: Major Activities, cloud providers undertake different tasks for the provisioning of the various service models.

For SaaS, the cloud provider deploys, configures, maintains, and updates the operation of the software applications on a cloud infrastructure so that the services are provisioned at the expected service levels to cloud consumers. The provider of SaaS assumes most of the responsibilities in managing and controlling the applications and the infrastructure, while the cloud consumers have limited administrative control of the applications.

For PaaS, the cloud provider manages the cloud infrastructure for the platform, and provisions tools and execution resources for the platform consumers to develop, test, deploy, and administer applications. Consumers have control over the applications and possibly the hosting environment settings, but cannot access the infrastructure underlying the platform including network, servers, operating systems, or storage.

For IaaS, the cloud provider provisions the physical processing, storage, networking, and other fundamental computing resources, as well as manages the hosting environment and cloud infrastructure for IaaS consumers. Cloud consumers deploy and run applications, have more control over the hosting environment and operating systems, but do not manage or control the underlying cloud infrastructure (e.g., the physical servers, network, storage, hypervisors, etc.).

The activities of cloud providers can be discussed in greater detail from the perspectives of *Service Deployment, Service Orchestration, Cloud Service Management, Security* and *Privacy.*

4.3.1 SERVICE DEPLOYMENT

As identified in the NIST cloud computing definition, a cloud infrastructure may be operated in one of the following deployment models: *public cloud, private cloud, community cloud*, or *hybrid cloud.* For the details related to the controls and management in the cloud, we refer readers to the NIST Special Publication 800-146, *NIST Cloud Computing Synopsis and Recommendations.*

A public cloud is one in which the cloud infrastructure and computing resources are made available to the general public over a public network. A public cloud is owned by an organization selling cloud services and serves a diverse pool of clients.

For private clouds, the cloud infrastructure is operated exclusively for a single organization. A private cloud gives the organization exclusive access to and usage of the infrastructure and computational resources. It may be managed either by the organization or by a third party, and may be implemented at the organization's premise (i.e., *on-site private clouds*) or outsourced to a hosting company (i.e., *outsourced private clouds*).

Similar to private clouds, a community cloud may be managed by the organizations or by a third party, and may be implemented at the customer's location (i.e., *on-site community cloud*) or outsourced to a hosting company (i.e., *outsourced community cloud*). However, a community cloud serves a set of organizations that have common security, privacy, and compliance considerations, rather than serving a single organization as does a private cloud.

A hybrid cloud is a composition of two or more cloud deployment models (private, community, or public) that remain unique entities but are bound together by standardized or proprietary technology that enables data and application portability. As discussed in this section, both private clouds and community clouds can be either implemented on-site or outsourced to a third party. Therefore, each constituent cloud of a hybrid cloud can be one of the five variants.

4.3.2 SERVICE ORCHESTRATION

Service orchestration refers to the arrangement, coordination, and management of cloud infrastructure to provide the optimizing capabilities of cloud services, as a cost-effective way of managing IT resources, as dictated by strategic business requirements. Figure 5 shows the general requirements and processes for cloud providers to build each of the three service models.

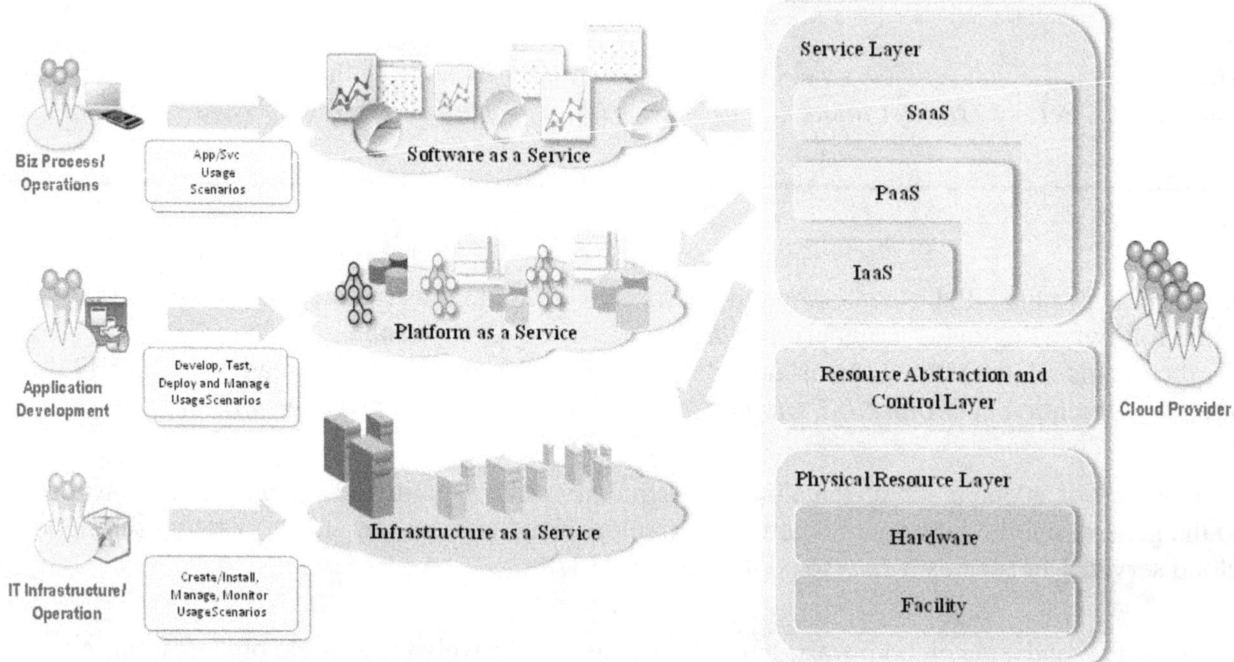

Figure 5 – Cloud Provider: Service Orchestration

A three-layered framework is identified for a generalized cloud system in Figure 5. The top layer is the service layer, where a cloud provider defines and provisions each of the three service models. This is where cloud consumers consume cloud services through the respective cloud interfaces.

The middle layer is the resource abstraction and control layer. This layer contains the system components that a cloud provider uses to provide and manage access to the physical computing resources through software abstraction. The layer typically includes software elements such as hypervisors, virtual machines, virtual data storage, and other resource abstraction and management components needed to ensure efficient, secure, and reliable usage. While virtual machine technology is commonly used at this layer, other means of providing the necessary software abstractions are not precluded. This layer provides "cloud readiness" with the five characteristics defined in the NIST definition of cloud computing.

The lowest layer in the framework is the physical resource layer, which includes all the physical computing resources. This layer includes hardware resources, such as computers (CPU and memory), networks (routers, firewalls, switches, network links, and interfaces), storage components (hard disks), and other physical computing infrastructure elements. It also includes facilities resources, such as heating, ventilation, and air conditioning (HVAC), power, communications, and other aspects of the physical plant.

Note that in this framework, the horizontal positioning of layers implies a stack in which the upper layer has a dependency on the lower layer. The resource abstraction and control layer build virtual cloud resources on top of the underlying physical resource layer and support the service layer where cloud services interfaces are exposed. The three service models can be built either on top of one another (i.e., SaaS built upon PaaS and PaaS built upon IaaS) or directly upon the underlying cloud infrastructure. For example, a SaaS application can be implemented and hosted on virtual machines from IaaS or directly on top of cloud resources without using IaaS.

4.3.3 CLOUD SERVICE MANAGEMENT

Cloud Service Management includes all of the service-related functions that are necessary for the management and operation of those services required by or proposed to cloud consumers. As illustrated in Figure 6, cloud service management can be described from the perspective of *business support, provisioning and configuration,* and from the perspective of *portability and interoperability* requirements.

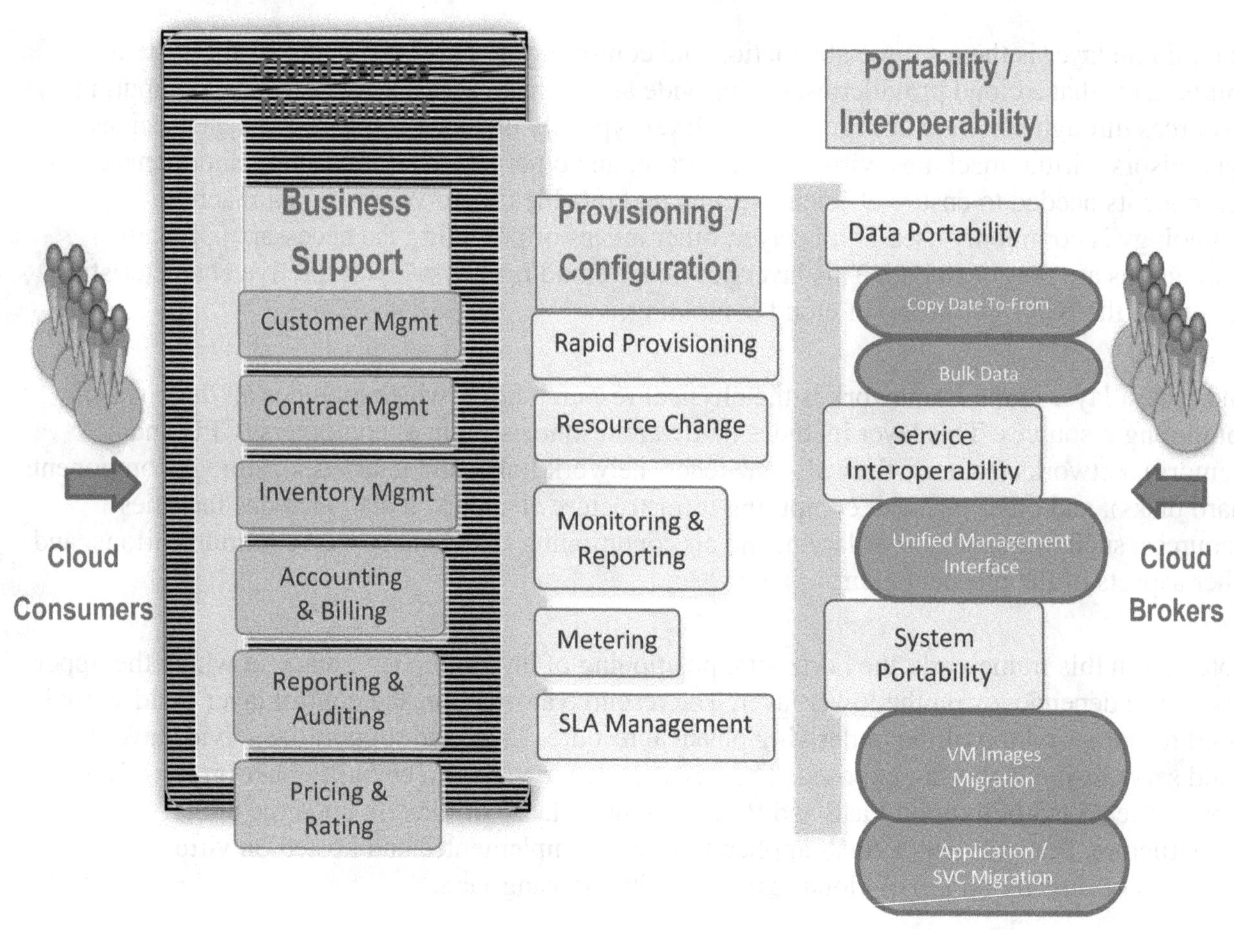

Figure 6 – Cloud Provider: Cloud Service Management

4.3.4 SECURITY

"As the Federal Government moves to the cloud, it must be vigilant to ensure the security and proper management of government information to protect the privacy of citizens and national security" (by Vivek Kundra, Federal Cloud Computing Strategy, February 2011.) In July 2012, the U.S. Department of Defense released a Cloud Computing Strategy, which stated "the Department has specific cloud computing challenges that require careful adoption considerations, especially in areas of cybersecurity, continuity of operations, information assurance (IA), and resilience." Also, in November 2012, NIST published a White Paper – *Challenging Security Requirements for U.S. Government Cloud Computing Adoption*. This document provides an overview of the high-priority security challenges perceived by federal agencies as impediments to the adoption of cloud computing.

Security is a cross-cutting function that spans all layers of the reference architecture (see Figure 12 – The Combined Conceptual Reference Diagram), involving end-to-end security that ranges from physical security to application security, and in general, the responsibility is shared between cloud provider and federal cloud consumer. For example, the protection of the physical resource layer (see Figure 5 – Cloud Provider: Service Orchestration) requires physical security that denies unauthorized access to the building, facility, resource, or stored information. Cloud Providers should ensure that the facility hosting cloud services is secure and that the staff has proper background checks. When data or applications are moved to a cloud, Cloud Consumers ensure that the cloud offering satisfies the security requirements and enforces the compliance rules. Several U.S. government agencies provide computer security guidance, and that the cloud system should support the most up-to-date guidance. It is also important to note that security, compliance, and policy requirements are a function of the legal jurisdiction of the country in which the cloud services are provided and can vary from country to country. An independent audit (see Section 3.4) should be conducted to verify the compliance with regulations or security policies.

4.3.5 PRIVACY

Cloud providers should protect the assured, proper, and consistent collection, processing, communication, use, and disposition of personal information (PI) and personally identifiable information (PII) in the cloud system. PII is the information that can be used to distinguish or trace an individual's identity, such as name, social security number, biometric records, etc., alone, or when combined with other personal or identifying information that is linked or linkable to a specific individual, such as date and place of birth, mother's maiden name, etc. The CIO Council – Privacy Committee[14] has identified privacy and protection of collected PII as one of the federal government key business imperatives. Though cloud computing provides a flexible solution for shared resources, software, and information, it also poses additional privacy challenges to consumers using the clouds.

The Digital Government Strategy [15] issued by the Federal Chief Information Officer (CIO) on May 23, 2012 sets forth a new vision of how government is to connect with and provide services to the American people, harnessing the power of digital technology and enabling citizens and the federal workforce to securely access government digital information, data, and services anywhere, and

[14] https://cio.gov/about/committees/privacy-committee/

[15] *Digital Government: Building a 21st Century Platform to Better Serve the American People* (May 23, 2012), (Strategy) http://www.whitehouse.gov/sites/default/files/omb/egov/digital-government/digital-government.html

anytime (Recommendations). [16] The Federal CIO Council released *Recommendations for Standardized Implementation of Digital Privacy Controls* (Recommendations), which discusses three fundamental privacy controls: PII Inventory, Privacy Impact Assessment (PIA), and Privacy Notice. The Recommendations are that agencies identify and consider all PII that may be collected or otherwise exposed through a particular digital technology, analyze the privacy risks through the data life cycle by conducting and updating a PIA (as needed), and provide notice to individuals of when and how their PII will be collected, used, retained, and disclosed.

Furthermore, federal agencies should be aware of the privacy concerns associated with the cloud computing environment where data are stored on a server that is not owned or controlled by the federal government. Privacy impact assessment (PIA) can be conducted, as needed, to measure how well the cloud system conforms to applicable legal, regulatory, and policy requirements regarding privacy. A PIA can help federal agencies comply with applicable privacy laws and regulations governing an individual's privacy, and to ensure confidentiality, integrity, and availability of an individual's personal information at every stage of development and operation.

In furthering the milestone action goal of the Digital Government Strategy for addressing digital privacy, records retention, and security issues, the National Archives & Records Administration (NARA) has issued Electronic Records Management (ERM) guidance for digital content created, collected, or maintained by federal agencies [17]. NARA also serves as managing partner of the E-Government ERM Initiative, coordinating the development and issuance of enterprise-wide ERM tools and electronic information standards, to support the interoperability of federal agency record systems and improve customer service (e.g., digital records access). [18]

---

[16] *Recommendations for Standardized Implementation of Digital Privacy Controls* (December 2012), https://cio.gov/wp-content/uploads/downloads/2012/12/Standardized_Digital_Privacy_Controls.pdf

[17] http://www.archives.gov/records-mgmt/initiatives/erm-guidance.html

[18] http://www.archives.gov/records-mgmt/initiatives/erm-overview.html

4.4 CLOUD AUDITOR

A cloud auditor is a party that can conduct independent assessment of cloud services, information system operations, performance, and the security of a cloud computing implementation. A cloud auditor can evaluate the services provided by a cloud provider in terms of security controls, privacy impact, performance, and adherence to service level agreement parameters.

Auditing is especially important for federal agencies as "agencies should include a contractual section enabling third parties to assess security controls of cloud providers" (*by Vivek Kundra, Federal Cloud Computing Strategy, February 2011*). Security controls are the management, operational, and technical safeguards or countermeasures employed within an organizational information system to protect the confidentiality, integrity, and availability of the system and its information. For security auditing, a cloud auditor can make an assessment of the security controls in the information system to determine the extent to which the controls are implemented correctly, operating as intended, and producing the desired outcome with respect to the security requirements for the system. The security auditing should include the verification of the compliance with regulation and security policy.

4.5 CLOUD BROKER

The NIST Reference Architecture, SP 500-292, [19] defines a Cloud Broker as an entity that manages the use, performance, and delivery of cloud services, and negotiates relationships between Cloud Providers and Cloud Consumers. As cloud computing evolves, the integration of cloud services may become too complex for cloud Consumers to manage. In such cases, a Cloud Consumer may request cloud services from a Cloud Broker instead of directly contacting a Cloud Provider. Cloud Brokers provide a single point of entry for managing multiple cloud services. The key defining feature that distinguishes a Cloud Broker from a Cloud Service Provider is the ability to provide a single consistent interface to multiple differing providers, whether the interface is for business or technical purposes. In general, Cloud Brokers provide services in three categories:

Intermediation: A Cloud Broker enhances a given service by improving some specific capability and providing value-added services to cloud Consumers. The improvement can be managing access to cloud services, identity management, performance reporting, enhanced security, etc.

Aggregation: A Cloud Broker combines and integrates multiple services into one or more new services. The Broker provides data and service integration and ensures the secure data movement between the cloud Consumer and multiple cloud Providers.

---

[19] http://www.cloudcredential.org/images/pdf_files/nist%20reference%20architecture.pdf

Arbitrage: Service arbitrage is similar to service aggregation except that the services being combined/consolidated are not fixed. Service arbitrage means a Broker has the flexibility to choose services from multiple service Providers.

A Cloud Broker may provide:

1. Business and relationship support services (business intermediation), and

2. Technical support service (aggregation, arbitrage, and technical intermediation), with a key focus on handling interoperability issues among multiple Providers.

4.6 CLOUD CARRIER

A cloud carrier acts as an intermediary that provides connectivity and transport of cloud services between cloud consumers and cloud providers. Cloud carriers provide access to consumers through network, telecommunication, and other access devices. For example, cloud consumers can obtain cloud services through network access devices, such as computers, laptops, mobile phones, mobile Internet devices (MIDs), etc. The distribution of cloud services is normally provided by network and telecommunication carriers or a *transport agent*, where a transport agent refers to a business organization that provides physical transport of storage media such as high-capacity hard drives. Note that a cloud provider will set up service level agreements (SLAs) [20] with a cloud carrier to provide services consistent with the level of SLAs offered to cloud consumers, and may require the cloud carrier to provide dedicated and encrypted connections between cloud consumers and cloud providers.

---

[20] SLAs are agreements under the umbrella of the overall cloud computing contract between a CSP and a cloud consumer. SLAs define acceptable service levels to be provided by the CSP to its customers in measurable terms. The ability of a CSP to perform at acceptable levels is consistent among SLAs, but the definition, measurement and enforcement of this performance varies widely among CSPs. A cloud consumer should ensure that CSP performance is clearly specified in all SLAs, and that all such agreements are fully incorporated, either by full text or by reference, into the CSP contract. [Source: *Creating Effective Cloud Computing Contracts for the Federal Government – Best Practices for Acquiring IT as a Service* https://cio.gov/wp-content/uploads/downloads/2012/09/cloudbestpractices.pdf

5 CLOUD COMPUTING USE CASES

Cloud computing use cases describe the consumer goals and actions for using cloud computing service offerings. Analyzing business and technical cloud computing use cases and the applicable standards provides an intuitive, utility-centric perspective for identifying requirements for all actors in the use case. This section leverages the business and technical use case outputs from other NIST Cloud Computing Program Working Groups. Section 8 presents an analysis regarding whether existing cloud-related standards fulfill key aspects of the use case for USG cloud consumers and highlights where the gaps for standardizations exist.

5.1 BUSINESS USE CASES

The Target Business Use Case Working Group produced a template for documenting specific use cases. This template includes a section titled "Concept of Operations" in which "Current System" and "Desired Cloud Implementation" states are described. The template also gathers information about integration with other systems, security requirements, and both local and remote network access considerations. A set of business use cases was collected describing candidate USG agency cloud deployments. The stories captured in these business use cases help to identify business drivers behind the adoption of cloud computing in USG agencies, provide background information on the relevant usage context, and expose general agency consumer concerns and issues through specific scenarios.

These use cases thus helped to document key technical requirements for USG cloud-related standards in the areas of security, interoperability, and portability studied for the formulation of this roadmap. Efforts are now underway to document similar requirements with respect to other key considerations, such as accessibility and performance of federal cloud-based business systems and services.

The "Cloud First" [21] directive provided by the Federal CIO is a more general expansion of this analysis to multiple interacting current systems and cloud implementations. This expansion is intended to support evolving business processes as further cloud deployments are implemented.

[21] 25 Point Implementation Plan to Reform Federal Information Technology Management http://www.dhs.gov/sites/default/files/publications/digital-strategy/25-point-implementation-plan-to-reform-federal-it.pdf

5.2 TECHNICAL USE CASES

The SAJACC Working Group has analyzed the output of the Business Use Case group, along with other community-provided documents and inputs, and produced a set of detailed cloud computing technical use case scenarios. These technical use cases captured and describe in detail the requirements, inputs, outputs, and failure and success conditions of cloud operations. They provide descriptions of how users or groups of users, called "actors," interact with one or more cloud computing resource systems to achieve specific goals, such as "how to copy data objects into a cloud," or "instantiate a virtual machine within a specific security context."

The mapping from the high-level business use cases to the SAJACC technical use cases allows a detailed understanding of ways in which the business operational stories of specific agency consumers identify specific technical requirements. Such requirements, as expressed in SAJACC technical use cases, are then well suited to demonstrate the applicability of cloud computing software or standards. For example, the business use case of an agency consumer's move of its virtualized computing infrastructure to an IaaS cloud vendor identifies "*Virtual Machine (VM) control: manage virtual machine instance state*" as a technical requirement to be met.

The SAJACC group has gathered detailed examples from U.S. federal agencies and analyzed them in terms of these technical use case scenarios. The results from this effort, along with demonstrations presented to the SAJACC group meetings, have been used to elucidate applicability of standards and the presence of standardization gaps in this current document. The rest of this section drives through the high-level business use cases to the general technical requirements expressed and analyzes where cloud standards help address these requirements.

5.3 DEPLOYMENT SCENARIO PERSPECTIVE

The "Cloud First" business use case requires more complex interactions between USG agency cloud consumer and cloud providers. There are three generic scenarios from which interaction scenarios are derived, as shown in Figure 7.

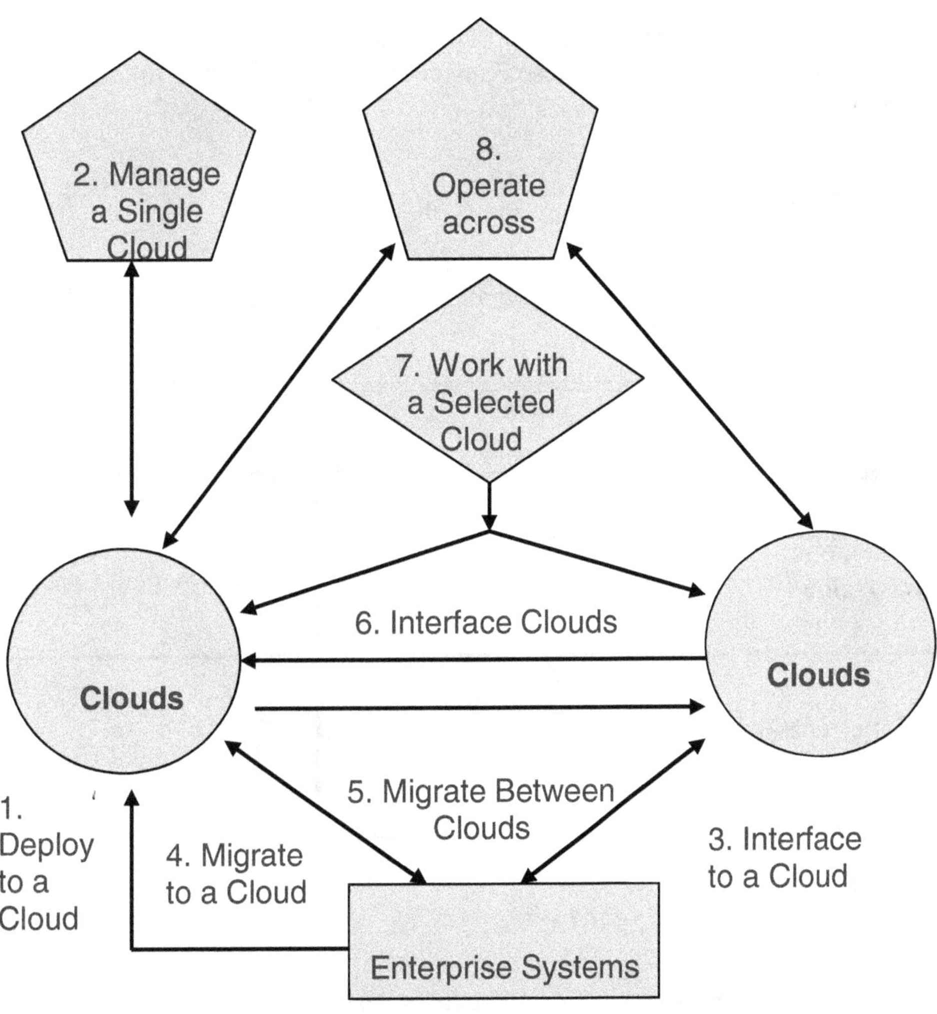

Figure 7 – High-Level Generic Scenarios

Single Cloud System

Scenario 1: Deployment on a single cloud system
Scenario 2: Manage resources on a single cloud system
Scenario 3: Interface enterprise systems to a single cloud system
Scenario 4: Enterprise systems migrated or replaced on a single cloud system

Multiple Cloud Systems (serially, one at a time)

Scenario 5: Migration between cloud systems
Scenario 6: Interface across multiple cloud systems
Scenario 7: Work with a selected cloud system

Multiple Cloud Systems – (simultaneously, more than one at a time)
Scenario 8: Operate across multiple cloud systems

These technical use cases must also be analyzed in the context of their deployment models and the resultant way cloud actors must interact. These considerations identify two fundamental dimensions to the spectrum of cloud computing use cases:

- Centralized vs. Distributed, and
- Within vs. Crossing Trust Boundaries

These deployment cases will drive the requirements for cloud standards. They can be identified through the following matrix:

	a.) Within Trust Boundary	b.) Crossing Trust Boundary
1.) Centralized i.e., one administrative cloud domain	Deployment Case 1A	Deployment Case 1B
2.) Distributed, i.e., crossing administrative cloud domains	Deployment Case 2A	Deployment Case 2B

Table 2 – Deployment Cases for High Level Scenarios

Deployment Case 1: In the centralized deployment cases, there is one cloud provider under consideration at a time. Each cloud provider may service multiple cloud consumers. Each cloud consumer has a simple client-provider interaction with the provider.

Deployment Case 1A: This deployment case is typically a private cloud within a single administrative domain and trust boundary wherein policy and governance can be enforced by nontechnical means. Use cases within this deployment case may require standards to support the following basic technical requirements:

- Simple, consumer-provider authentication;
- VM management;
- Storage management;
- SLAs and performance/energy monitoring;
- Service discovery;
- Workflow management;

- Auditing; and
- Virtual organizations in support of community cloud use cases.

Deployment Case 1B: This deployment case is typically (commercial) public cloud within a single administrative domain but is outside of any trust boundary that a client could use to enforce policy and governance. Clients must rely on the cloud provider to enforce policy and governance through technical means that are "baked into" the infrastructure. Use cases within this deployment case may require standards to support the following additional technical requirements:

- SLAs in support of governance requirements, e.g., national or regional regulatory compliance;
- Stronger authentication mechanisms, e.g., Public Key Infrastructure (PKI) Certificates, etc.;
- Certification of VM isolation through hardware and hypervisor support;
- Certification of storage isolation through hardware support; and
- Data encryption.

Deployment Case 2: In the distributed deployment cases, a single cloud consumer has an application that may be distributed across two or more cloud providers and administrative domains simultaneously. While the cloud consumer may have simple consumer-provider interactions with their application and the providers, more complicated Peer-to-Peer ("P2P") interactions may be required -- between both the consumer and provider and also between the providers themselves.

Deployment Case 2A: This deployment case is typically a federated cloud of two or more administrative cloud domains, but where the cloud providers can agree "out of band" how to mutually enforce policy and governance -- essentially establishing a common trust boundary. Use cases within this deployment case may require standards to support the following basic technical requirements:

- P2P service discovery;
- P2P SLA and performance monitoring;
- P2P workflow management;
- P2P auditing;
- P2P security mechanisms for authentication, authorization; and
- P2P virtual organization management.

Deployment Case 2B: This deployment case is typically a hybrid cloud where applications cross a private-public trust boundary, or even span multiple public clouds, where both administrative domains and trust boundaries are crossed. Consumers must rely on the cloud provider to enforce policy and governance through technical means that are "baked into" the infrastructure. Applications and services may be distributed and need to operate in a P2P manner. Use cases within this deployment case will require all the standards of the other deployment cases, in addition to the following more extensive technical requirements:

- P2P SLAs in support of governance requirements.

The use cases presented in this section will be analyzed with regards to their possible *deployment scenarios* to determine their requirements for standards. This analysis will subsequently be used to evaluate the likelihood of each of these deployment cases. Clearly the expected deployment of these use cases across the different deployment cases will not be uniform. This non-uniformity will assist in producing a *prioritized roadmap* for cloud standards. Likewise, in reviewing existing standards, these use cases – in conjunction with their possible deployment cases – will be used to identify and prioritize *gaps* in available standards.

Based on this analysis, note that Scenarios 1 through 4 could, in fact, be deployed on either a private cloud or a public cloud. Hence, the different standards noted in deployment cases 1A and 1B will be required. Scenarios 5, 6, and 7 (below) all involve the notion of the serial use of multiple clouds. Presumably these different clouds, used serially, could be either private or public. Hence, deployment cases 1A and 1B would also apply, but there are additional requirements to achieve portability, e.g., Application Programming Interface (API) commonality. Finally, Scenario 8 could involve a federated/community cloud or a hybrid cloud. Hence, deployment cases 2A and 2B would apply here.

To summarize the detailed technical use cases for this analysis, the following areas of technical requirements are common across all scenarios:

Scenarios	Technical Requirements
1.	Creating, accessing, updating, deleting data objects in cloud systems;
2.	Moving VMs and virtual appliances between cloud systems;
3.	Selecting the best IaaS vendor for private externally hosted cloud system;
4.	Tools for monitoring and managing multiple cloud systems;
5.	Migrating data between cloud systems;
6.	Single sign-on access to multiple cloud systems;
7.	Orchestrated processes across cloud systems;
8.	Discovering cloud resources;
9.	Evaluating SLAs and penalties; and
10.	Auditing cloud systems.

Table 3 – Scenarios and Technical Requirements

6 CLOUD COMPUTING STANDARDS

Standards are already available in support of many of the functions and requirements for cloud computing described in Section 3 and Section 4. While many of these standards were developed in support of pre-cloud computing technologies, such as those designed for web services and the Internet, they also support the functions and requirements of cloud computing. Other standards are now being developed in specific support of cloud computing functions and requirements, such as virtualization.

To assess the state of standardization in support of cloud computing, the NIST Cloud Computing Standards Roadmap Working Group has compiled an Inventory of Standards Relevant to Cloud Computing http://collaborate.nist.gov/twiki-cloud-computing/bin/view/CloudComputing/StandardsInventory.

6.1 INFORMATION AND COMMUNICATION TECHNOLOGIES (IT) STANDARDS LIFE CYCLE

Figure 8 is a high-level conceptualization of ways in which IT standards are developed and methods by which standards-based IT products, processes, and services are deployed. This figure is not meant to imply that these processes occur sequentially. Many of the processes illustrated can and should occur concurrently. Some of these processes (e.g., reference implementations, product / process / service / test tools development, testing, deployment) can and usually do also occur outside of the SDO process. These processes provide input and feedback to improve the standards, profiles, test tools, and associated stages of product development.

Cloud computing development has been characterized by its emergence during a period in which extremely interconnected and fast-moving product cycles have led to an explosion of innovation that strains the conventional SDO-based standards development process. While this is a rapidly changing area, cloud computing is not unique in this respect, and several other examples exist in history of similar periods of rapid change followed by standardization. In the long run, the processes that drive IT standards development are likely to follow historical precedent as over-arching requirements begin to become clear, and as standards emerge from such processes to fill these requirements. We therefore expect conformance testing, conformity assessment, and other processes related to the maturity and adoption of standards to emerge. Some evidence of this maturity is already starting to become manifest in the cloud standards landscape.

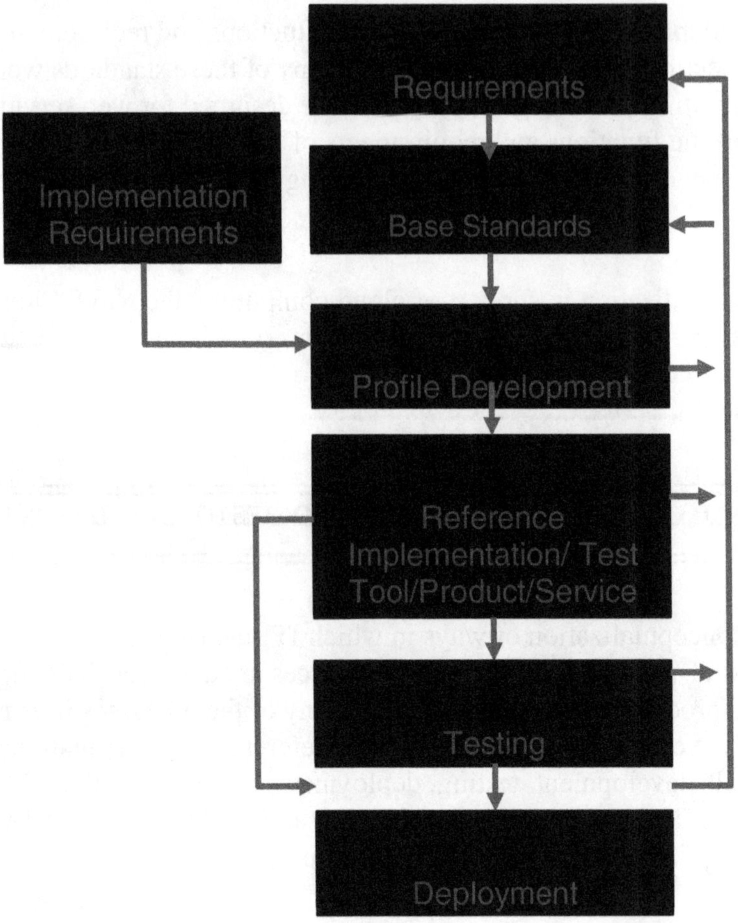

Figure 8 – IT Standards Life Cycle

6.2 THE ROLE OF CONFORMITY ASSESSMENT TO STANDARDS

Conformity assessment activities form a vital link between standards, which define necessary characteristics or requirements, and the products, services, and systems. Conformity assessment enables buyers, sellers, consumers, and regulators to have confidence that products, processes, and systems sourced in the global market meet specific requirements. It is the demonstration that specified requirements relating to a product, process, or system are fulfilled.

The characteristics of cloud computing including on-demand, self-service, and resource pooling among multiple tenants need to be considered when establishing conformance regimes for cloud services. For example, conformance testing may need to be done online against a production system that includes data and applications owned and controlled by other tenants. But privacy may preclude inspection of system logs, and it may not be possible to inspect the source code or run debugging tools. Test harnesses may not be able to be built into the service but may need to be run as a client to the cloud service. It may be necessary to establish an account in order to access the service for testing.

6.2.1 CONFORMITY ASSESSMENT ACTIVITIES

Conformity assessment procedures provide a means of ensuring that the products, services, systems, persons, or bodies have certain required characteristics, and that these characteristics are consistent from product to product, service to service, system to system, etc. Conformity assessment can include: supplier's declaration of conformity, sampling and testing, inspection, certification, management system assessment and registration, the accreditation of the competence of those activities, and recognition of an accreditation program's capability. A specific conformity assessment scheme or program may include one or more conformity assessment activities. While each of these activities is a distinct operation, they are closely interrelated.

Conformity assessment activities can be performed by many types of organizations or individuals. Conformity assessment can be conducted by: (1) a first party, which is generally the supplier or manufacturer; (2) a second party, which is generally the purchaser or user of the product; (3) a third party, which is an independent entity that is generally distinct from the first or second party and has no interest in transactions between the two parties; and (4) the government, which has a unique role in conformity assessment activities related to regulatory requirements.

Attestation consists of the issuance of a statement, based on a decision following review, that fulfillment of specified requirements has been demonstrated. First-party and third-party attestation activities are distinguished by the terms declaration (first party), certification (third party), and accreditation (third party).

A supplier's declaration of conformity is a first party (e.g., supplier) attestation that a product, process, service, etc., conforms to specified requirements. These requirements may include normative documents such as standards, guides, technical specifications, laws, and regulations. The supplier may conduct the testing or contract with a third party to do the testing. The test results are evaluated by the supplier, and when all requirements are met, the supplier issues a formal statement that the product is in conformance to the requirements. A statement that the product meets specific requirements can be included in the product documentation or other appropriate location, and the test results and other supporting documentation can be made available when requested.

Certification is a third-party attestation related to products, services, systems, etc. Accreditation is a third-party attestation related to a conformity assessment body conveying formal demonstration of its competence to carry out specific conformity assessment tasks. Testing laboratory accreditation provides formal recognition that a laboratory is competent to carry out specific tests or calibrations or types of tests or calibrations.

Rapidly advancing technology and increased international competition make it essential that suppliers have an opportunity to utilize all available options to minimize costs and ensure that the time to bring a product to market is at a minimum. Conformity assessment is an important aspect in the development of product, processes and services, but this assessment does add costs and time to the development cycle.

6.2.2 GOVERNMENT USE OF CONFORMITY ASSESSMENT SYSTEMS

Federal conformity-assessment activities are a means of providing confidence that the products, services, systems, etc. regulated or purchased by federal agencies, or that are the subject of federal assistance programs, have the required characteristics and/or perform in a specified manner. The NTTAA directs NIST to coordinate federal, state, and local government standards and conformity assessment activities with those of the private sector, with the goal of eliminating unnecessary duplication and complexity in the development and promulgation of conformity assessment requirements and measures. Conformity assessment that leverages existing private-sector programs can help lower the cost of implementation for agencies, and also provide added impetus for innovation and competitiveness. Numerous federal agencies are engaged in conformity assessment activities. In addition, as part of its role mandated by the NTTAA, many federal programs utilize NIST support to help design and implement appropriate and effective conformity assessment programs.

6.2.3 VISUALIZATION OF CONFORMITY ASSESSMENT PROCESSES

Figure 9 – Conformity Assessment Infrastructure provides an overview of the range of activities that can occur in conformity assessment and the relationships between them.

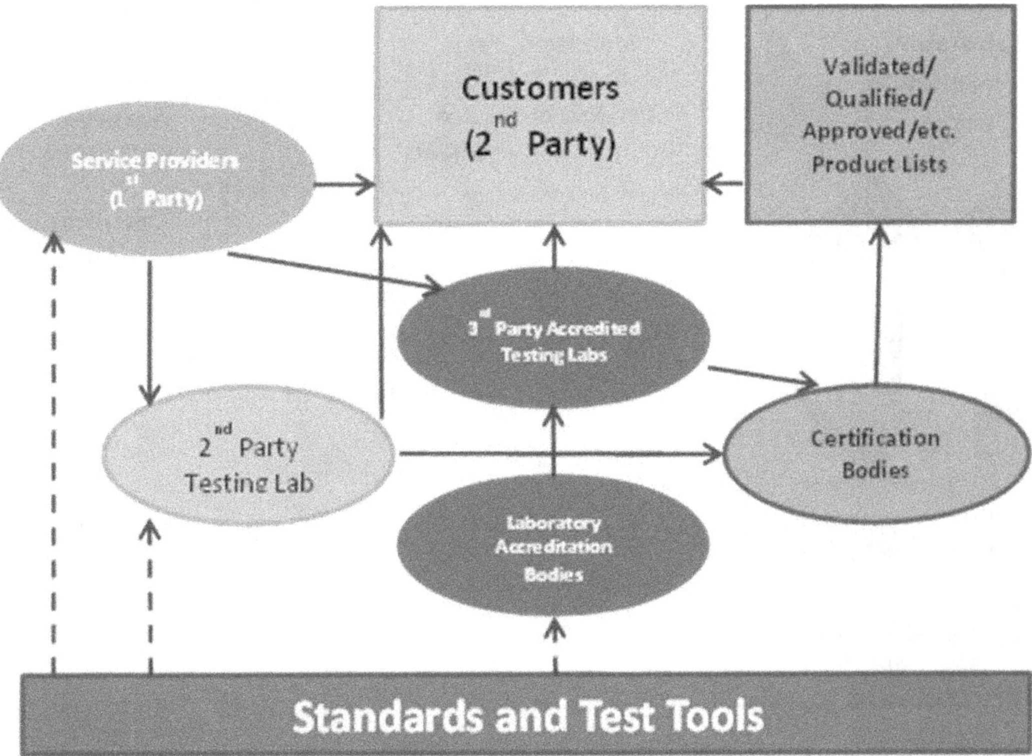

Figure 9 – Conformity Assessment Infrastructure

Figure 10 – Accreditation Process shows the relationships for the laboratory accreditation process. The key aspect of the process is the identification of the standards, test methods, test tools, and other technical requirements by the procurement agency as they apply to the products, services, systems, etc., to be tested.

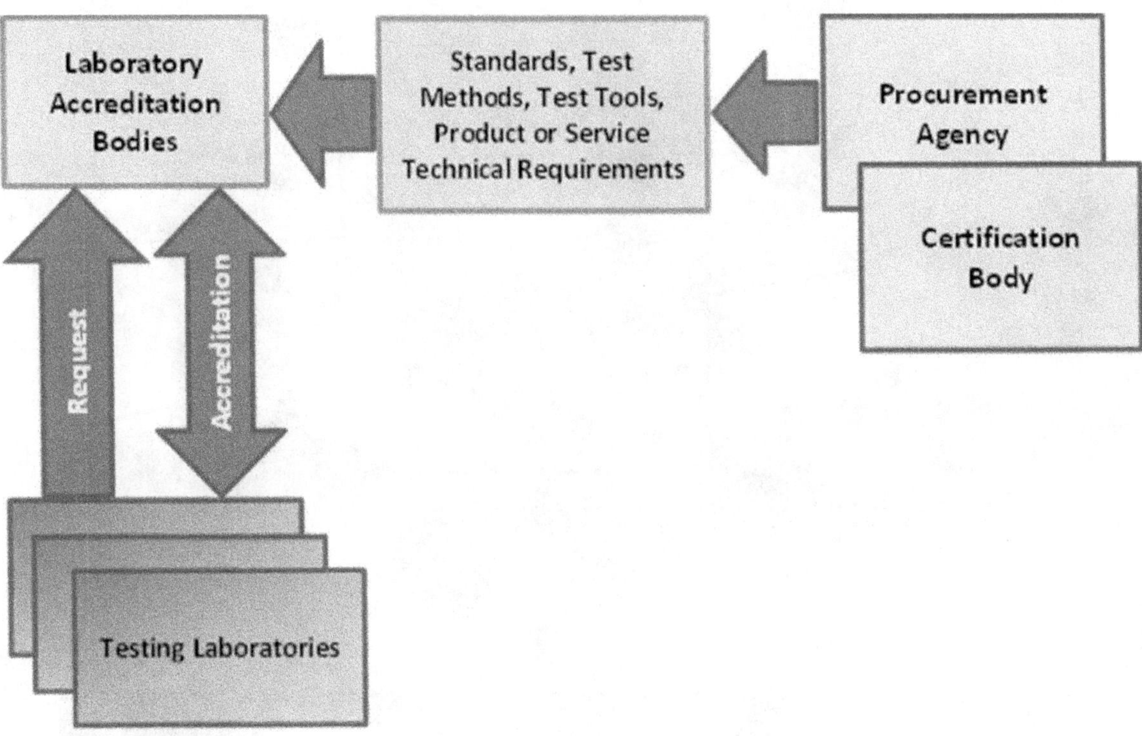

Figure 10 – Accreditation Process

An example of a conformity assessment system using accredited testing laboratories and certification is provided in Figure 11 – Assessment Process. The process starts with the submission by the supplier of the product, service, or system to a third-party accredited testing laboratory. The laboratory tests the product in accordance with the requirements and forwards the test results to the supplier. If the results are satisfactory to the supplier, they will be forwarded by the laboratory to the validation authority designated by the procurement agency in coordination with the qualified products list (QPL) owner. These experts will review the test reports and will make a recommendation as to their acceptance to the QPL owner. If the QPL owner agrees with the recommendations, the product, service, or system will be listed.

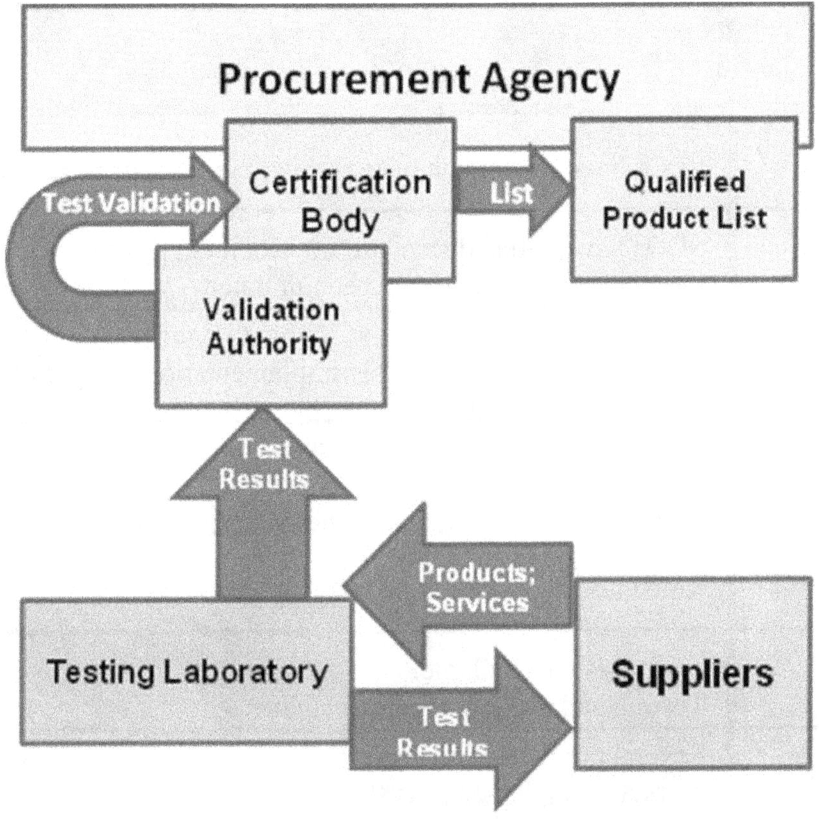

Figure 11 – Assessment Process

6.2.4 CURRENT STATE OF CONFORMITY ASSESSMENT IN CLOUD COMPUTING

As described elsewhere in this document, standards specific to cloud computing are beginning to emerge, and several aspects of the conformance testing and conformity assessment processes described above are also starting to take place, conducted by a variety of organizations. In some cases, such as the CDMI, OCCI, OVF, and CIMI standards discussed below, industry-sponsored testing events and “plug-fests” are being advertised and conducted with participation from a variety of vendors and open source projects and community-based developers. In other cases, either the standards are not yet mature enough to permit such testing, or the participants have not yet exposed the conformity assessment processes to public view.

6.3 CATEGORIZING THE STATUS OF STANDARDS

Innovation in IT means that IT standards are constantly being developed, approved, and maintained. Revisions to previous editions of standards may or may not be backward-compatible. Table 4 – Standards Maturity Model provides an indication of the maturity level of a standard. Some SDOs require two or more implementations before final approval of a standard. Such implementations may or may not be commercially available products or services. In other cases, an SDO may be developing standards while commercial products or services are already being sold that conform to early drafts. (In such cases, companies take on the risk of creating products or services that may not conform to the final standard.)

Maturity Level	Definition
No Standard	SDOs have not initiated any standard development projects.
Under Development	SDOs have initiated standard development projects. Open source projects have been initiated.
Approved Standard	SDO-approved standard is available to public. Some SDOs require multiple implementations before final designation as a "standard."
Technically Stable	The standard is stable and its technical content is mature. No major revisions or amendments are in progress that will affect backward compatibility with the original standard.
Reference Implementation	Reference implementation is available.
Testing	Test tools are available. Testing and test reports are available.
Commercial Availability	Several products/services from different vendors exist on the market to implement this standard.
Market Acceptance	Widespread use by many groups. De facto or de jure market acceptance of standards-based products/services.
Sunset	Newer standards (revisions or replacements) are under development.

Table 4 – Standards Maturity Model

6.4 CLOUD COMPUTING STANDARDS FOR INTEROPERABILITY AND PORTABILITY

Cloud platforms should make it possible to securely and efficiently move data in, out, and among cloud providers and to make it possible to port applications from one cloud platform to another. Data may be transient or persistent, structured or unstructured and may be stored in a file system, cache, relational or non-relational database. Cloud interoperability means that data can be processed by different services on different cloud systems through common specifications. Cloud portability means that data can be moved from one cloud system to another and that applications can be ported and run on different cloud systems at an acceptable cost.

The migration path to cloud computing should preserve existing investments in technologies which are appropriate to the cloud system, and that enables the coexistence and interoperability of on-premises software and cloud services. Additionally, the migration to a cloud system should enable various multiple cloud platforms seamless access between and among various cloud services, to optimize the cloud consumer expectations and experience.

Cloud interoperability allows seamless exchange and use of data and services among various cloud infrastructure offerings and to use the data and services exchanged to enable them to operate effectively together.

Cloud portability allows two or more kinds of cloud infrastructures to seamlessly use data and services from one cloud system and be used for other cloud systems.

For example, a financial application might use a petabyte of data, but that data might be securely housed in a single cloud database, making it relatively easy to port. On the other hand, a customer relationship management (CRM) application running in the cloud system might process only a terabyte of data but which is shared among thousands of users; moving the CRM application – and all its distributed data – from one cloud system to another would be more challenging. Overall, functionality of cloud interoperability is preferable.

6.4.1 CLOUD STANDARDS FOR INTEROPERABILITY

Interoperability may be assessed in terms of the NIST Cloud Computing Reference Architecture at the IaaS, PaaS, and SaaS levels. Each of these levels, which may be combined in any particular cloud service or product in practice, presents special considerations, and as a result, the standards landscape is intrinsically unique and specific to each level.

At the IaaS level, two published standard sets exist that are applicable, the Open Cloud Computing Interface (OCCI) specification set from Open Grid Forum and the Cloud Infrastructure Management Interface (CIMI) set from the Distributed Management Task Force (DMTF). OCCI, published in early 2011, is slightly more general in formulation and presents a generic boundary-level protocol for achieving RESTful control of a target infrastructure within the given boundary. It has been applied to virtual machine instantiation and control, provision and discovery of network features and other internal features, and has an extensible, self-describing feature set. CIMI, more recently developed and published in late 2012, has a tightly described calling sequence and also provides features that conform to DMTF's Common Information Model (CIM). Each of these standard sets has seen significant uptake, and several available cloud system products either already implement or plan to implement at least one of them. While these IaaS standard sets are so far separate, OGF and DMTF have stated that they have a work register in place and that they continue to discuss the possibility of merging these efforts in the future.

In PaaS applications, an extensive ecosystem of vendor-specific products that are not interchangeable has emerged. A recent effort to produce a PaaS-specific standard [22] has been started by the OASIS Cloud Application Management Protocol (CAMP) technical committee, with support from several industry participants, and is making rapid progress towards producing a workable specification.

In the case where a SaaS application is consumed through a web browser, there may be many standards that are used to achieve interoperability between what is essentially a web server and the user's browser, such as IP (v4, v6), TCP, HTTP, SSL/TLS, HTML, XML, REST, Atom, AtomPub, RSS, and JavaScript/JSON. None of these web standards are cloud-specific, and these same standards are being used in many web browser-based management interfaces.

Where data is acted on by multiple services, cloud or otherwise, there are various standards that enable interoperability. Also important are interoperability standards for distributed applications such as SOAP, WS-* and ebXML. Other standards that can be used for interoperability between cloud services include OpenID, Odata, CDMI, AMQP, and XMPP. Most important for interoperability are canonical data content formats, typically today expressed using XML standards. Such standard canonical formats include "nouns," i.e., the data objects being acted on, but also (implicitly or explicitly) the "verbs," i.e., the actions that a receiving service may or should take on such a data object (e.g., Sync, Process, Get, Show, etc.). While "verbs" may be somewhat generic, such canonical formats are in general specific to a particular domain.

Various standards exist corresponding to different application domains (e.g., OAGi BODs for business documents or ODF and OOXML for office productivity documents). Also important is the stack of interoperability standards for interfaces, packaging, and transport such as SOAP, WS-* and ebXML. Since the SaaS area is so wide-ranging, cloud-based SaaS products are likely to continue to exercise and to explore the full range of Internet protocols for their communication and interfaces. It is more likely that data formats and metadata-based interchange methods will be standardized in cloud system products rather than having SaaS interfaces themselves converge. Examples of such

[22] ID Cloud-PaaS https://www.oasis-open.org/committees/download.../IDCloud-paas-v1c.odt

data format description standardization include the Data Format Description Language (DFDL) from OGF and the Cloud Data Management Interface (CDMI) data-container metadata model of the Storage Networking Industry Association (SNIA). As the cloud computing landscape is currently heavily populated by vendor-specific formats, such general-purpose standardization efforts may be crucial to achieving interoperability at the SaaS level.

As appropriate, some of these interfaces will be tested and analyzed by NIST to validate their capabilities against the list of cloud computing use cases. Opportunities will also be made available for the vendor and open source community to demonstrate the applicability of standards and APIs to the defined NIST SAJACC cloud computing technical use cases.

6.4.2 CLOUD COMPUTING STANDARDS FOR PORTABILITY

Over the last year, much progress has been made on new standards in this area. Open Virtualization Format (OVF) from the Distributed Management Task Force (DMTF), for example, was developed to address portability concerns between various virtualization platforms. It consists of metadata about a virtual machine image or groups of images that can be deployed as a unit. It provides a mechanism to package and deploy services as either a virtual appliance or used within an enterprise to prepackage known configurations of a virtual machine image or images. It may contain information regarding the number of CPUs, memory required to run effectively, and network configuration information. It also can contain digital signatures to ensure the integrity of the machine images being deployed along with licensing information in the form of a machine-readable EULA (End User License Agreement) so that it can be understood before the image(s) is deployed.

Significant progress has also been made in the creation of new standards focused on portability concerns at higher levels of abstraction such as the cloud service and application. Topology and Orchestration Services for Applications (TOSCA) from OASIS, for example, was developed to address portability concerns between services and applications that may be required to be deployed on different cloud providers and platforms due to reasons such as regulatory concerns, changing business and market factors, or evolving technical requirements. TOSCA provides a machine-readable language to describe the relationships between components, requirements, and capabilities. The intent is to facilitate service and life cycle management of services and applications in IaaS, PaaS, and SaaS environments while enabling the specification of life cycle operations at that level of abstraction, e.g., deploy, patch, shutdown, in a cloud platform and provider independent fashion. As of February 2013, the TOSCA specification had completed a 30-day public review. A primer, which includes a chapter on the relationship between OVF and TOSCA is under development.

A future direction of workloads data and metadata standardization is to help improve the automation of inter-cloud system workload deployment. Concepts such as standardized SLAs, sophisticated inter-virtual machine network configuration and switching information, and software license information regarding all of the various components that make up the workload are possibilities.

Another aspect of portability in the cloud system is that of storage and data (including metadata) portability between cloud systems, for example, between storage cloud services and between compatible application services in SaaS and PaaS layers.

Cloud storage services may be seen as a special class of application service, where the storage metadata (as distinct from the stored data content) is the application data that a receiving cloud system must be able to process. For cloud storage services, as much of the actual data movement needs to be done in bulk moves of massive numbers of objects, retaining the data organization (into containers, for example) and retaining the associated metadata are main portability requirements.

Data portability between cloud application services requires standard formats and protocols. The canonical data formats commonly involved in portability scenarios may be focused on widely used application categories, for example, email or office productivity, or on specific formats used by particular domains of use, for example, science or medical domains. Popular methods for interchange of data in cloud systems generally leverage representations in either JSON or XML formats, and are often customized to particular fields of use through standards.

Standards are key to achieving portability. Building on existing standards and specifications that are known to work and are in widespread use and documenting how the standards are implemented, allows developers to continue to use their chosen development languages and tools as they build for cloud systems. This keeps migration costs and risks low by enabling organizations to leverage their IT staff's current skills, and by providing a secure migration path that preserves existing investments. Examples of languages, tools, and standards that are common in the cloud system include programming languages such as Java, C#, PHP, Python and Ruby; Internet protocols for service access such as REST, SOAP, and XML; federated identity standards for service authentication such as SAML and OAuth; and standards for managing virtualized environments.

Standards continue to rapidly evolve in step with technology. Hence, cloud standards may be at different stages of maturity and levels of acceptance. OVF, for example, is an open standard for packaging and distributing virtual appliances. Originally offered as a proprietary format to the DMTF, OVF was first published in March 2009, and subsequently adopted in August 2010 as a national standard by the American National Standards Institute (ANSI).

When a provider claims conformance with any other standard, it should cite the specific version and publish implementation, errata, and testing notes. This will provide the transparency necessary for informed consumer choice, as well as ensure reasonably seamless technical interoperability between on-premises and cloud virtualized systems.

6.4.3 SUMMARY ON INTEROPERABILITY AND PORTABILITY

Substantial progress has been made by SDOs to develop standards that meet specific cloud computing requirements and use cases. There are now existing standards that support cloud service interoperability and data portability but gaps remain in the standards, specifically in the PaaS area, and current development efforts still need to mature. As cloud standards evolve, they will need to describe how services interoperate and how data can be readily ported between cloud offerings.

As cloud standards and IT standards that support cloud implementations change and evolve, the issues of governance and orchestration of cloud architectures will become more prevalent and simultaneously, how to 'standardize' a governance model will need to be updated. Governance of the cloud is analogous to the governance of Internet but rather than standardizing on packets of data, it is standardizing on how data and services are shared. Cloud standards will need to describe how services and data can be readily ported or interoperate between cloud offerings as seamless, efficient access to data and services across cloud providers will become the demand signal from customers. The SAJACC group has received and has begun analyzing input from several SDOs and from federal agencies with regard to this topic, including the area of service agreements and SLAs that is explored further in Section 6.6, "Cloud Standards for Performance".

6.5 CLOUD COMPUTING STANDARDS FOR SECURITY

As noted in SP 800-146, "the term cloud computing encompasses a variety of systems and technologies as well as service and deployment models, and business models". Cloud computing's unique attributes such as elasticity, rapid provisioning and releasing, resource pooling, multi-tenancy, broad-network accessibility, and ubiquity bring many benefits to cloud adopters, but also entails specific security risks associated with the type of adopted cloud and deployment mode. To accelerate the adoption of cloud computing, and to advance the deployment of cloud services, solutions coping with cloud security threats need to be addressed. Many of the threats that cloud providers and consumers face can be dealt with through traditional security processes and mechanisms such as security policies, cryptography, identity management, intrusion detection/prevention systems, and supply chain vulnerability analysis. However, risk management activities must be undertaken to determine how to mitigate the threats specific to different cloud models and to analyze existing standards for gaps that need to be addressed.

Securing the information systems and ensuring the confidentiality, integrity, and availability of information and information being processed, stored, and transmitted are particularly relevant as these are the high-priority concerns and present a higher risk of being compromised in a cloud computing system. Cloud computing implementations are subject to local physical threats as well as remote, external threats.

Consistent with other applications of IT, the threat sources include accidents, natural disasters that induce external loss of service, hostile governments, criminal organizations, terrorist groups, and malicious or unintentional vulnerabilities exploited through internal, external, authorized, or unauthorized access to the system. The complexity of the cloud computing architecture supporting three service types and four deployment models, and the cloud characteristics, specifically multi-tenancy, heighten the need to consider data and systems protection in the context of logical, physical boundaries and data flow separation.

Possible types of security challenges for cloud computing services include the following:

- Compromises to the confidentiality and integrity of data in transit to and from a cloud provider and at rest;
- Attacks which take advantage of the homogeneity and power of cloud computing systems to rapidly scale and increase the magnitude of the attack;
- A consumer's unauthorized access (through improper authentication or authorization, or exploit of vulnerabilities introduced maliciously or unintentionally) to software, data, and resources provisioned to, and owned by another authorized cloud consumer;
- Increased levels of network-based attacks that exploit software not designed for an Internet-based model and vulnerabilities existing in resources formerly accessed through private networks;
- Limited ability to encrypt data at rest in a multi-tenancy environment;
- Portability constraints resulting from the lack of standardization of cloud services application programming interfaces (APIs) that preclude cloud consumers to easily migrate to a new cloud service provider when availability requirements are not met;
- Attacks that exploit the physical abstraction of cloud resources and exploit a lack of transparency in audit procedures or records;
- Attacks that take advantage of known, older vulnerabilities in virtual machines that have not been properly updated and patched;
- Attacks that exploit inconsistencies in global privacy policies and regulations;
- Attacks that exploit cloud computing supply chain vulnerabilities to include those that occur while cloud computing components are in transit from the supplier to the cloud service provider;
- Insider abuse of their privileges, especially cloud provider's personnel in high risk roles (e.g. system administrators; and
- Interception of data in transit (man-in-the-middle attacks).

Some of the main security objectives for a cloud computing implementer should include:

- Protect consumers' data from unauthorized access, disclosure, modification or monitoring. This includes supporting identity management and access control policies for authorized users accessing cloud services. This includes the ability of a customer to make access to its data selectively available to other users.

- Prevent unauthorized access to cloud computing infrastructure resources. This includes implementing security domains that have logical separation between computing resources (e.g. logical separation of customer workloads running on the same physical server by VM monitors [hypervisors] in a multi-tenant environment) and using secure-by-default configurations.

- Deploy in the cloud web applications designed and implemented for an Internet threat model.

- Challenges to prevent Internet browsers using cloud computing from attacks to mitigate end-user security vulnerabilities. This includes taking measures to protect internet-connected personal computing devices by applying security software, personal firewalls, and patch maintenance.

- Include access control and intrusion detection and prevention solutions in cloud computing implementations and conduct an independent assessment to verify that the solutions are installed and functional. This includes traditional perimeter security measures in combination with the domain security model. Traditional perimeter security includes restricting physical access to network and devices; protecting individual components from exploitation through security patch deployment; setting as default most secure configurations; disabling all unused ports and services; using role-based access control; monitoring audit trails; minimizing privileges to minimum necessary; using antivirus software; and encrypting communications.

- Define trust boundaries between cloud provider(s) and consumers to ensure that the responsibilities to implement security controls are clearly identified.

- Implement standardized APIs for interoperability and portability to support easy migration of consumers' data to other cloud providers when necessary.

6.6 CLOUD COMPUTING STANDARDS FOR PERFORMANCE

There are numerous reasons why cloud computing standards for performance are needed in today's market. Consumers need to be able to objectively determine the costs and benefits of moving to cloud services; to validate claims of performance by cloud providers; and to objectively compare services from multiple providers in order to better meet a specific need.

Determining performance involves establishing a set of metrics that will provide a clear picture of how a given cloud service performs. This is complex due to the fact that specific metrics and standards will be needed for not only specific categories of services, but also due to the domains in which they are needed. For example, dealing with private healthcare data will need performance standards relating to both privacy and security. Standards might be needed for attributes that are associated with the service such as network performance. Additionally, standards are needed that measure attributes specific to cloud service such as virtual machine performance.

While not an exhaustive list, other potential performance aspects relevant to the cloud include:

- Management performance
- Benchmark performance
- Cloud service life cycle elements:
    - Negotiation performance
    - Instantiation performance
    - Termination performance
- Performance testing
    - Monitoring
    - Auditing

In the end, these performance standards will be of interest to many of the stakeholders involved in cloud computing. Cloud consumers and providers will use these standards and metrics as a basis for creating measurable and enforceable service level agreement contracts. Auditors will be able to measure performance for their customers. Cloud brokers will need these standards to ensure that their customer's specific needs are met. Cloud providers will be performing self-evaluations on their own offerings.

The topic of performance includes considerations related to monitoring, reporting, measuring, scaling, and right-sizing cloud resources to meet the expected or experienced demand. This area deserves careful consideration, as it relates directly to the factors that control the potential cost savings to the government from the use of cloud computing.

Performance can potentially be scaled to meet conditions of anticipated or real-world demand, within the parameters of a cloud service agreement. It is therefore crucial that such agreements contain all necessary parameters that relate to the conditions for delivery of the associated cloud service or product. Only by careful measurement and by proper anticipation of peak workload conditions, backed by appropriate service remedies, credits, or penalties and appropriate fallback arrangements, can true cost savings be realized with proper delivery of services.

Agencies using cloud services should be careful to include suitable performance, monitoring, and emergency metrics and conditions into the cloud service master agreement and associated SLA. These elements, reflecting the agencies given mission and goals, will help to ensure that each agency will pay only for needed services.

Cloud services are particularly well suited to deployment of automated terms and conditions for the delivery of these services. While the basic parameters, legal, and cost controls for cloud services require agency approval and human-mediated review, automated tools should be deployed where appropriate to ensure conditions such as failover in the event of cloud service component failure or compromise, and scaling to meet emergent needs or to grow or shrink service delivery according to cost and/or demand, and other relevant features.

Wherever possible, standards-based methods for monitoring, measuring, and scaling delivery of the resources to meet agency missions should be pursued.

6.6.1 CLOUD STANDARDS FOR SERVICE AGREEMENTS

At the moment, most cloud service agreements are expressed in human-readable terms for review by legal staff and management. Tools are increasingly available, however, for expression of service agreement conditions, remedies, and provisions that can be expressed in machine-readable terms and that can even serve as the basis for service templates that can be provisioned automatically, directly from the service agreement template.

Examples of these methods can be seen in several open source products based on the WS-Agreement and WS-Agreement-Negotiation specifications from OGF. Recent work from an inter-SDO joint task force led by TM Forum has also produced a white paper[23] describing the

[23] https://www.tmforum.org/WhitePapers/CloudMonetization/47730/article.html

considerations for end-to-end service agreement management specifically oriented towards management of multiple cloud service SLAs. The possibility of "TOSCA service template extension to support SLA management and possible mapping to SID information framework," is also discussed.

The TM Forum has developed a set of standards to help in the implementation and management of services that span multiple partners in a "multi-cloud" system. Organized as "packs", these standards focus on managing service level agreements between partners, and ensure consistency in the management of information across aggregated services with particular emphasis where these services cross multi-company boundaries. There are Business, Technical, and Accelerator Packs that have been published; these documents augment the Cloud Service Level Agreement Handbook (GB917) that was published by the TM Forum in April 2012. The TM Forum has also developed a series of documents working primarily with large-scale enterprises and ensuring that their best practice needs are met in the delivery of cloud services.

6.6.2 CLOUD STANDARDS FOR MONITORING

The situation with regard to cloud service monitoring is less well developed than for other areas due to the multiplicity of underlying products and the lack of a single set of well-defined monitoring and metric terms. To address this need, the NIST Cloud Computing Reference Architecture and Taxonomy group is developing a set of terms related to monitoring and metrics for service agreements, including SLAs.

The input from this group and from the TM Forum-led joint cross-SDO report discussed above will be used by the Business Use Case and SAJACC groups to develop use case scenarios that can be used to identify appropriate standards and standards gaps in this area.

ITU-T's establishment of a cloud computing resource management area of study, a roadmap for the area of study and the initiation of related supporting standards, is beginning to address the closure of some of the standards gaps in cloud computing monitoring. The roadmap outlines the standards that are needed in order to monitor the health, QoS, and reliability of cloud services that are based on the aggregation of services from one or more cloud service providers.

6.7 CLOUD COMPUTING STANDARDS FOR ACCESSIBILITY

Accessibility is relevant to cloud computing services at the application level where a human interacts with an application. This is where accessibility is measured. Therefore, many of the existing accessibility standards for ICT applications are relevant to cloud computing applications.

The U.S. Access Board is an independent federal agency devoted to accessibility for people with disabilities. The Access Board develops and maintains design criteria for the built environment, transit vehicles, telecommunications equipment, and for electronic and information technology. It also provides technical assistance and training on these requirements and on accessible design and enforces accessibility standards that cover federally funded facilities.

Section 508 of the Rehabilitation Act of 1973, as amended (29 U.S.C. 794d), requires that Federal employees with disabilities have access to and use of information and data that are comparable to the access and use by federal employees who are not individuals with disabilities. Section 508 also requires that individuals with disabilities, who are members of the public seeking information or services from a federal agency, have access to and use of information and data that are comparable to that provided to the public who are not individuals with disabilities. Both of these requirements must be met unless an undue burden would be imposed on the agency.

Section 508 standards that would be applicable for many cloud computing applications are: Subpart B -- Technical Standards 1194.21 Software applications and operating systems; § 1194.22 Web-based intranet and internet information and applications; and 1194.23 Telecommunications products. The Access Board is in the process of revising the Section 508 standards. This is the first major revision since the standards were initially published in 2001. The initial product oriented approach to requirements is being replaced with a more functional approach. The Access Board plans to reference the W3C's Web Content Accessibility Guidelines (WCAG) 2.0 (http://www.w3.org/TR/WCAG20/), which is an international voluntary consensus guideline.

Additional voluntary consensus standards that may be applicable to cloud computing applications are: ISO 9241-20:2008, Ergonomics of human-system interaction -- Part 20: Accessibility guidelines for information/communication technology (ICT) equipment and services; ISO 9241-171:2008, Ergonomics of human-system interaction -- Part 171: Guidance on software accessibility; ANSI/HFES 200 Human Factors Engineering of Software User Interfaces (Parts 1, 2, and 3); and ISO/IEC 24751-1:2008, Information technology -- Individualized adaptability and accessibility in e-learning, education and training -- Part 1: Framework and reference model.

The White House released a memorandum *Strategy Plan for Improving Management of Section 508 of the Rehabilitation Act,* January 24, 2013 [24]. The strategic plan provides a comprehensive and structured approach to further improve agencies' management of the requirements of Section 508. The objective is to ensure that all electronic and information technology (EIT) that is developed, procured, maintained, or used by the federal government is accessible, as required by Section 508 of the Rehabilitation Act of 1973.

[24] www.whitehouse.gov/sites/default/files/omb/procurement/memo/strategi-plan-508-compliance.pdf

7 CLOUD COMPUTING STANDARDS MAPPING

One approach to cloud computing standards mapping is to map relevant standards using the conceptual model and the cloud computing taxonomy from the NIST Cloud Computing Reference Architecture and Taxonomy Working Group. As presented in Figure 12, the cloud computing conceptual model is depicted as an integrated diagram of system, organizational, and process components. The cloud computing taxonomy produced by the same working group has provided further categorizations for the security, interoperability, and portability aspects for cloud computing.

While many standards are generally relevant to these cloud computing areas, the following sections will map those specifically relevant cloud standards and capture their standard maturity status in a tabular format. The online cloud standards inventory (as described in Section 5) will be the place to maintain and track other relevant standards. Some standards may apply to more than one category from the cloud taxonomy and therefore may be listed more than once.

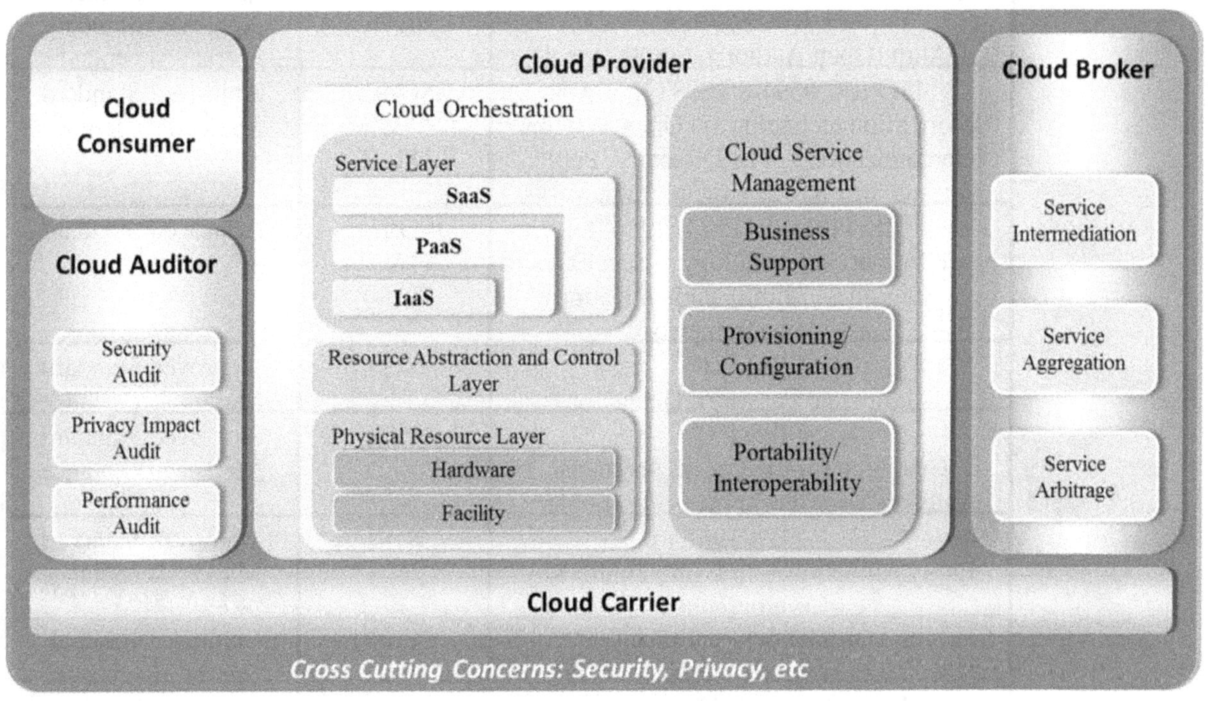

Figure 12 – The Combined Conceptual Reference Diagram

7.1 SECURITY STANDARDS MAPPING

The following tables map security standards to various security categories and list the status (ref: Section 6.3/ Table 4 – Standards Maturity Model). Some of the listed standards apply to more than one category and are therefore listed more than once.

Categorization	Available Standards	SDO	Status
Authentication & Authorization	RFC 5246 Secure Sockets Layer (SSL)/ Transport Layer Security (TLS)	IETF	Approved Standard Market Acceptance
	RFC 3820: X.509 Public Key Infrastructure (PKI) Proxy Certificate Profile	IETF	Approved Standard Market Acceptance
	RFC5280: Internet X.509 Public Key Infrastructure Certificate and Certificate Revocation List (CRL) Profile	IETF	Approved Standard Market Acceptance
	RFC 5849 OAuth (Open Authorization Protocol)	IETF	Approved Standard Market Acceptance
	ISO/IEC 9594-8:2008 I X.509 Information technology -- Open Systems Interconnection -- The Directory: Public-key and attribute certificate frameworks	ISO/IEC & ITU-T	Approved Standard Market Acceptance
	ISO/IEC 29115 I X.1254 Information technology -- Security techniques -- Entity authentication assurance framework	ISO/IEC & ITU-T	Approved Standard
	FIPS 181 Automated Password Generator	NIST	Approved Standard Market Acceptance
	FIPS 190 Guideline for the Use of Advanced Authentication Technology Alternatives	NIST	Approved Standard Market Acceptance
	FIPS 196 Entity Authentication Using Public Key Cryptography	NIST	Approved Standard Market Acceptance
	OpenID Authentication	OpenID	Approved Standard Market Acceptance
	eXtensible Access Control Markup Language (XACML)	OASIS	Approved Standard Market Acceptance
	Security Assertion Markup Language (SAML)	OASIS	Approved Standard Market Acceptance

Table 5 – Security Standards: Authentication and Authorization

Categorization	Available Standards	SDO	Status
Confidentiality	RFC 5246 Secure Sockets Layer (SSL)/ Transport Layer Security (TLS)	IETF	Approved Standard Market Acceptance
	Key Management Interoperability Protocol (KMIP)	OASIS	Approved Standard Market Acceptance
	XML Encryption Syntax and Processing	W3C	Approved Standard Market Acceptance
	FIPS 140-2 Security Requirements for Cryptographic Modules	NIST	Approved Standard Testing Market Acceptance
	FIPS 185 Escrowed Encryption Standard (EES)	NIST	Approved Standard Market Acceptance
	FIPS 197 Advanced Encryption Standard (AES)	NIST	Approved Standard Testing Market Acceptance
	FIPS 188 Standard Security Label for Information Transfer	NIST	Approved Standard Market Acceptance

Table 6 – Security Standards: Confidentiality

Categorization	Available Standards	SDO	Status
Integrity	XML signature (XMLDSig)	W3C	Approved Standard Market Acceptance
	FIPS 180-4 Secure Hash Standard (SHS)	NIST	Approved Standard Market Acceptance
	FIPS 186-4 Digital Signature Standard (DSS)	NIST	Approved Standard Market Acceptance
	FIPS 198-1 The Keyed-Hash Message Authentication Code (HMAC)	NIST	Approved Standard Market Acceptance

Table 7 – Security Standards: Integrity

Categorization	Available Standards	SDO	Status
Identity Management	X.idmcc Requirement of IdM in Cloud Computing	ITU-T	Under Development
	FIPS 201-1 Personal Identity Verification (PIV) of Federal Employees and Contractors	NIST	Approved Standard Market Acceptance
	Service Provisioning Markup Language (SPML)	OASIS	Approved Standard
	Web Services Federation Language (WS-Federation) Version 1.2	OASIS	Approved Standard
	WS-Trust 1.3	OASIS	Approved Standard
	Security Assertion Markup Language (SAML)	OASIS	Approved Standard Market Acceptance
	OpenID Authentication 1.1	OpenID Foundation	Approved Standard Market Acceptance

Table 8 – Security Standards: Identity Management

Categorization	Available Standards	SDO	Status
Security Monitoring & Incident Response	ISO/IEC WD 27035-1 Information technology -- Security techniques -- Information security incident management -- Part 1: Principles of incident management	ISO/IEC	Under Development
	ISO/IEC WD 27035-3 Information technology -- Security techniques -- Information security incident management -- Part 3: Guidelines for CSIRT operations	ISO/IEC	Under Development
	ISO/IEC WD 27039; Information technology -- Security techniques -- Selection, deployment and operations of intrusion detection systems	ISO/IEC	Under Development
	ISO/IEC 18180 Information technology - Specification for the Extensible Configuration Checklist Description Format (XCCDF) Version 1.2 (NIST IR 7275)	ISO/IEC	Approved Standard Market Acceptance
	X.1500 Cybersecurity information exchange techniques	ITU-T	Approved Standard Market Acceptance
	X.1520: Common vulnerabilities and exposures	ITU-T	Approved Standard
	X.1521 Common Vulnerability Scoring System	ITU-T	Approved Standard
	PCI Data Security Standard	PCI	Approved Standard Market Acceptance
	FIPS 191 Guideline for the Analysis of Local Area Network Security	NIST	Approved Standard Market Acceptance

Table 9 – Security Standards: Security Monitoring & Incident Response

Categorization	Available Standards	SDO	Status
Security Controls	Cloud Controls Matrix Version 1.3	CSA	Approved Standard
	ISO/IEC 27001:2005 Information Technology – Security Techniques Information Security Management Systems Requirements	ISO/IEC	Approved Standard
	ISO/IEC WD TS 27017 Information technology -- Security techniques -- Information security management - Guidelines on information security controls for the use of cloud computing services based on ISO/IEC 27002	ISO/IEC	Under Development
	ISO/IEC 27018 Code of Practice for Data Protection Controls for Public Cloud Computing Services	ISO/IEC	Under Development
	ISO/IEC 1st WD 27036-4 Information technology – Security techniques – Information security for supplier relationships – Part 4: Guidelines for security of cloud services	ISO/IEC	Under Development

Table 10 – Security Standards: Security Controls

Categorization	Available Standards	SDO	Status
Security Policy Management	ATIS-02000008 Trusted Information Exchange (TIE)	ATIS	Approved Standard Commercially Available
	FIPS 199 Standards for Security Categorization of Federal Information and Information Systems	NIST	Approved Standard Testing Market Acceptance
	FIPS 200 Minimum Security Requirements for Federal Information and Information Systems	NIST	Approved Standard Testing Market Acceptance
	ISO/IEC 27002 Code of practice for information security management	ISO/IEC	Approved Standard Market Acceptance
	eXtensible Access Control Markup Language (XACML)	OASIS	Approved Standard Market Acceptance

Table 11 – Security Standards: Security Policy Management

Categorization	Available Standards	SDO	Status
Availability	ATIS-02000009 Cloud Services Lifecycle Checklist	ATIS	Approved Standard
	ISO/PAS 22399:2007 Societal security - Guideline for incident preparedness and operational continuity management	ISO	Approved Standard Market Acceptance

Table 12 – Security Standards: Availability

7.2 INTEROPERABILITY STANDARDS MAPPING

As discussed in Section 6.3, the interoperability of cloud services can be categorized by the management and functional interfaces of the cloud services. Many existing IT standards contribute to the interoperability between cloud consumer applications and cloud services, and between cloud services themselves. There are standardization efforts that are specifically initiated to address the interoperability issues in the cloud system. These cloud specific standards are listed in Table 13 – Interoperability Standards.

Categorization	Available Standards	SDO	Status
Service Interoperability	Cloud Infrastructure Management Interface (CIMI)	DMTF	Approved Standard
	IEEE P2301, Draft Guide for Cloud Portability and Interoperability Profiles (CPIP)	IEEE	Under Development
	IEEE P2302, Draft Standard for Intercloud Interoperability and Federation (SIIF)	IEEE	Under Development
	Y.3520 Cloud computing framework for end to end resource management.	ITU-T	Approved Standard
	Cloud Application Management Platform (CAMP)	OASIS	Under Development
	Open Cloud Computing Interface (OCCI)	OGF	Approved Standard
	Data Format Description Language (DFDL)	OGF	Approved Standard
	Topology and Orchestration Specification or Cloud Applications (TOSCA),Version 1.0 Committee Specification Draft 06 / Public Review Draft 01	OASIS	Under Development
	Cloud Data Management Interface (CDMI) [Also approved as ISO/IEC 17826:2012, Information technology – Cloud Data Management Interface (CDMI)]	SNIA	Approved Standard Market Acceptance Commercially Available

Table 13 – Interoperability Standards

7.3 PORTABILITY STANDARDS MAPPING

As discussed in Section 6.4, portability issues in the cloud system include workload and data portability. While some of the cloud computing workload portability issues are new, many of existing data and metadata standards were developed before the cloud computing era. The following table focuses on cloud-specific portability standards.

Categorization	Available Standards	SDO	Status
Data Portability	Cloud Data Management Interface (CDMI)	SNIA	Approved Standard Market Acceptance Commercially Available
System Portability	Open Virtualization Format (OVF), OVF 1.0 [Also approved as INCITS 469-2010 & ISO/IEC 17203: 2011]	DMTF	Approved Standard Market Acceptance Commercial Availability
	Open Virtualization Format (OVF), OVF 2.0	DMTF	Approved Standard
	IEEE P2301 Draft Guide for Cloud Portability and Interoperability Profiles (CPIP)	IEEE	Under Development
	Topology and Orchestration Specification for Cloud Applications (TOSCA),Version 1.0 Committee Specification Draft 06 / Public Review Draft 01	OASIS	Under Development

Table 14 – Portability Standards

7.4 PERFORMANCE STANDARDS MAPPING

As discussed in Section 6.6, performance standards are needed for cloud service agreements and for cloud service monitoring, Table 15 – Performance Standards provides a list of current standards that may be considered.

Categorization	Available Standards	SDO	Status
Service Agreements	Topology and Orchestration Specification for Cloud Applications (TOSCA),Version 1.0 Committee Specification Draft 06 / Public Review Draft 01	OASIS	Under Development
	GB917 SLA Management Handbook, Release 3.1	TM Forum	Approved Standard
	GB963 Cloud SLA Application Note, Version 1.2	TM Forum	Approved Standard
	TR178 Enabling End-to-End Cloud SLA Management, Version 0.4	TM Forum	Approved Standard
	TR194 Multi-Cloud Service Management Accelerator Pack - Introduction, Release 1.0	TM Forum	Approved Standard
	TR195 Multi-Cloud Service Management Pack - Business Guide, Release 1.0	TM Forum	Approved Standard
	TR196 Multi-Cloud Service Management Pack - Technical Guide, Release 1.0	TM Forum	Approved Standard
	TR197 Multi-Cloud Service Management Pack – SLA Business Blueprint	TM Forum	Approved Standard
	TR198 Multi-Cloud Service Management Pack – Developer Primer	TM Forum	Approved Standard

Table 15 – Performance Standards

7.5 ACCESSIBILITY STANDARDS MAPPING

As discussed in Section 6.7, adherence to Section 508 accessibility standards would be required for many federal cloud computing applications. The Section 508 standards are being revised and are incorporating international voluntary consensus standards. The following table lists accessibility standards, which may be relevant for federal cloud computing applications.

Categorization	Available Standards	SDO	Status
Accessibility	Section 508 standards (Technical Standards 1194.21 Software applications and operating systems; § 1194.22 Web-based intranet and internet information and applications; and 1194.23 Telecommunications products)	US Access Board	Approved Standard Market Acceptance Under Revision
	W3C Web Content Accessibility Guidelines (WCAG) 2.0	W3C	Approved Standard Market Acceptance
	ISO 9241-20:2008, Ergonomics of human-system interaction -- Part 20: Accessibility guidelines for information/communication technology (ICT) equipment and services	ISO/IEC	Approved Standard
	ISO 9241-171:2008, Ergonomics of human-system interaction -- Part 171: Guidance on software accessibility	ISO/IEC	Approved Standard
	ISO/IEC 24751-1:2008, Information technology -- Individualized adaptability and accessibility in e-learning, education and training -- Part 1: Framework and reference model	ISO/IEC	Approved Standard
	ANSI/HFES 200 Human Factors Engineering of Software User Interfaces (Parts 1, 2, and 3)	ANSI	Approved Standard

Table 16 – Accessibility Standards

8 ANALYZING USE CASES TO IDENTIFY STANDARDS GAPS

There are several facets of cloud service interfaces that are candidates for standardization including:

- Management APIs;
- Data Exchange Formats;
- Federated Identity and Security Policy APIs;
- Resource Descriptions; and
- Data Storage APIs.

With these candidate areas in mind, the following business use cases can be analyzed with regard to their possible deployment modes (as discussed in Section 4.3) to identify required standards. This analysis, in conjunction with the NIST Cloud Standards Inventory, enables the availability of relevant existing and emerging standards to be evaluated. Where no suitable standards of any kind exist, this is a gap. The priority of the standards or requirements in question is also identified.

8.1 USE CASE: CREATING, ACCESSING, UPDATING, DELETING DATA OBJECTS IN CLOUD SYSTEMS

Benefits: Cross-cloud system applications

Deployment Mode Considerations: Basic Create-Read-Update-Delete (CRUD) operations on data objects will primarily be done between a single client and provider, and should observe any required standards for authentication and authorization.

Standardization Needed: Standard interfaces to metadata and data objects

Possible Standards: CDMI from SNIA

8.2 USE CASE: MOVING VMS, VIRTUAL APPLIANCES, SERVICES, AND APPLIANCES BETWEEN CLOUDS

Benefits: Migration, Hybrid Clouds, Disaster Recovery, Cloudbursting

Deployment Mode Considerations: When moving a VM out of one cloud system and into another as two separate actions, conceivably two different ID management systems could be used. When moving VMs in a truly hybrid cloud, however, federated ID management standards will be needed.

Standardization Needed: Common VM description format, common service and application description format

Possible Standards: OVF from DMTF, TOSCA from OASIS, OpenID, Oauth

8.3 USE CASE: SELECTING THE BEST IAAS CLOUD VENDOR, PUBLIC OR PRIVATE

Benefits: Provide cost-effective reliable deployments

Deployment Mode Considerations: When considering hybrid or distributed (inter)cloud deployments, uniform and consistent resource, performance, and policy descriptions are needed.

Standardization Needed: Resource and performance requirements description languages.

Possible Standards: For basic resource descriptions, DMTF CIM and OGF GLUE are candidates. Other, more extensive description languages for performance or policy enforcement are to be determined. For Master Service Agreements and Service Level Agreements, WS-Agreement and WS-Agreement-Negotiation (WS-AG, WS-AN) from OGF; for cloud application and service level description of attributes, relationships, requirements, and capabilities, TOSCA from OASIS.

8.4 USE CASE: PORTABLE TOOLS FOR MONITORING AND MANAGING CLOUD SYSTEMS

Benefits: Simplifies operations as opposed to individual tools for each cloud

Deployment Mode Considerations: Monitoring and managing are separate but closely related tasks. The standards required will differ depending on whether the monitoring and managing must be done across trust boundaries or across distributed environments.

Standardization Needed: Standard monitoring and management interfaces to IaaS resources

Possible Standards: Cloud IaaS management standards include CIMI from DMTF and OCCI from OGF; OCCI has also been successfully applied to management of aggregated federated cloud systems. PaaS APIs vary widely, but CAMP from OASIS has begun standardization work in this area. SaaS standardization on data formats and exchange protocols may be possible. Basic monitoring standards exist, such as the Syslog Protocol (IETF RFC 5424), which can be used with the Transport Layer Security (TLS) Transport Mapping for Syslog (IETF RFC 5425). Basic management standards include the Cloud Management WG from DMTF, and OCCI from OGF.

- An Overview of the IETF Network Management Standards (IETF RFC 6632)
- Simple Network Management Protocol or SNMP (IETF RFC 3411)
- IP Flow Information eXport or IPFIX (IETF RFC 5101)
- Network Configuration Protocol or NETCONF (IETF RFC 6241)
- WS-AG and WS-AN for expression of service agreement monitoring parameters and units and for expression of remedy terms and negotiation parameters.

8.5 USE CASE: MOVING DATA BETWEEN CLOUD SYSTEMS

Benefits: Migration between cloud systems, cross-cloud application, and B2B integration

Deployment Mode Considerations: Migrating data from one cloud system to another in two separate moves through the client is a simpler case. Migrating data directly from one cloud system to another will require standards for federated identity, delegation of trust, and secure third-party data transfers.

Standardization Needed: Standard metadata/data formats for movement between cloud systems

Standardized query languages (e.g., for NoSQL for IaaS)

Possible Standards: AS4, OAGIS, NoSQL, GridFTP, DFDL, CDMI

8.6 USE CASE: SINGLE SIGN-ON ACCESS TO MULTIPLE CLOUD SYSTEMS

Benefits: Simplified access, cross-cloud applications

Deployment Mode Considerations: Single sign-on can mean using the same credentials to access different cloud systems independently at different times. Single sign-on to access an inter-cloud application that spans multiple cloud systems will require federated identity management, delegation of trust, and virtual organizations.

Standardization Needed: Federated identity, authorization, and virtual organizations

Possible Standards: OpenID, OAuth, SAML, WS-Federation and WS-Trust, CSA outputs; Virtual Organization Management System (VOMS) from OGF.

8.7 USE CASE: ORCHESTRATED PROCESSES ACROSS CLOUD SYSTEMS AND ENTERPRISE SYSTEMS

Benefits: Direct support for necessarily distributed systems

Deployment Mode Considerations: This use case is inherently distributed and across trust boundaries. This can be generally termed federated resource management and is a central concept in the grid computing community. The term inter-cloud can also be used to denote this concept.

Standardizations Needed: To address this use case completely, an entire set of capabilities need to be standardized, e.g.:

- Infrastructure services;
- Execution Management services;
- Data services;
- Resource Management services;
- Security services;
- Self-management services; and
- Information services.

Possible Standards: SOA standards (such as WS-I) and grid standards (such as the OGSA WSRF Basic Profile, OGF GFD-R-P.072) exist that cover these areas, but issues around stateful resources, callbacks/notifications, and remote content lifetime management has caused these to be eclipsed by the simplicity of Representational State Transfer (REST). Hence, standard, REST-based versions of these capabilities must be developed. Such work is being done in several organizations, including the IEEE.

DMTF and OGF. The OGF Distributed Computing Infrastructure Federations Working Group (DCI Federal [DCIfed]-WG) is addressing two usage scenarios: (1) delegation of workload from one domain into the other, covering job description, submission, and monitoring; and (2) leasing of resources, including resource definition, provisioning, and monitoring. Existing standards to support this include WS-Agreement, Job Submission Description Language, GLUE, OGSA Basic Execution Service, OCCI, and Usage Record. Specific business application data formats may be supported by OASIS.

Workflow and workflow engines will also need standardization and adoption in the cloud arena. BPEL is one existing standard but extensions might be needed to efficiently support scientific and engineering workflows.

8.8 USE CASE: DISCOVERING CLOUD RESOURCES

Benefits: Selection of appropriate cloud systems for applications

Deployment Mode Considerations: To support inter-cloud resource discovery, secure federated catalog standards are needed.

Standardization Needed: Description languages for available resources, Catalogue interfaces

Possible Standards: This use case addresses two areas of standardization: (1) description languages for the resources to be discovered, and (2) the discovery APIs for the discovery process itself. Some existing standards and tools cover both areas. RDF is a standard formalism for describing resources as triples consisting of subject-predicate-object. The Dublin Core is a small fundamental set of text elements for describing resources of all types. It is commonly expressed in RDF. Since the Dublin Core is a "core" set, it is intended to be extensible for a broad range of application domains.

Such work is being pursued by the Dublin Core Metadata Initiative. ebXML Registry Information Model (ebRIM) actually defines both a description language and a discovery method, ebXML Registry Services (ebRS).

ID-WSF also defines both a discovery information model and discovery services that cover federated identity and access management. LDAP is an existing standard that has been used to build catalogue and discovery services, but issues might occur with regards to read vs. write optimization. UDDI is another existing standard from OASIS. A third existing standard is CSW from OGC that uses ebRIM. While this was originally developed to support geospatial applications, it is widely used in distributed catalogues that include services. All of these existing standards need to be evaluated for suitability for cataloguing and discovery of cloud resources and services.

8.9 USE CASE: EVALUATING SLAS AND PENALTIES

Benefits: Selection of appropriate cloud resources

Deployment Mode Considerations: SLAs will be primarily established between a single client and provider, and should observe any required standards for authentication, authorization, and non-repudiation. The need for SLAs between a single client but across multiple providers will be much less common. The difficulty in effectively implementing distributed SLAs will also discourage their development.

Standardization Needed: SLA description language

Possible Standards: WS-Agreement (GFD.107) defines a language and a protocol for advertising the capabilities of service providers and creating agreements based on creational offers, and for monitoring agreement compliance at runtime. This is supported by WS-AgreementNegotiation (OGF), which defines a protocol for automated negotiation of offers, counter offers, and terms of agreements defined under WS-Agreement-based service agreements.

8.10 USE CASE: AUDITING CLOUD SYSTEMS

Benefits: Ensure regulatory compliance. Verify information assurance.

Deployment Mode Considerations: Auditing will be done primarily between a single client and provider, and should observe any required standards for authentication, authorization, integrity, and non-repudiation.

Standardization Needed: Auditing standards and verification check lists

Possible Standards: CSA Cloud Audit. Relevant informational work can be found in Guidelines for Auditing Grid Certificate Authorities (OGF GFD.169).

8.11 END-TO-END: CLOUD RESOURCE MANAGEMENT USE CASE

Benefits: Supports customer service in a multi-cloud service provider environment.

Deployment/Management Mode Considerations: This use case involves the management of end-to-end health and QoS of the services offered by a cloud service provider that involves the integration of several base services offered by multiple cloud service providers, forming composite cloud services and applications.

Standardizations Needed: A framework for multi-cloud resource and service management that support the manageability for a single cloud service as well as for multiple cloud services

Possible Standards: In order for the composite cloud computing services to work effectively, all the prerequisite services within the multi-cloud service system must function properly, and when a problem occurs, the service must be restored rapidly and easily. In this use case, there are the two types of connection paths, namely Service Delivery Path and Service Management Path. When the cloud consumer is experiencing a problem with an application service and contacts a cloud service provider support center, the cloud service provider should have visibility into the health and welfare of the cloud service provider application service, its underlying cloud infrastructure, as well as the local service provider's network management systems relevant to the voice application service (i.e., end-to-end cloud resource management). Standards are needed that would offer ways to build such end-to-end and manageable multi-cloud solutions.

9 USG PRIORITIES TO FILL CLOUD COMPUTING STANDARDS GAPS

Cloud computing is the result of evolutions of distributed computing technologies, enabled by advances in fast and low-cost networks, commoditized faster hardware, practical high-performance virtualization technologies, and maturing interactive web technologies. Cloud computing continues to leverage the maturity of these underlying technologies, including many standard-based technologies and system architecture components. As the previous sections of the cloud computing standards survey show, the majority of cloud system relevant standards are from these pre-cloud era technologies.

In the meantime, there are emerging challenges in some areas in cloud computing that have been addressed by technology vendors and service providers' unique innovations. New service model interactions and the distributed nature in resource control and ownership in cloud computing have resulted in new standards gaps. Some of these gaps are introduced by new service model interactions and the distributed nature of resource control and ownership in cloud computing and some are pre-cloud computing era technology standardization gaps that are now brought to the forefront.

In this section, first, we use the cloud computing conceptual model from NIST Cloud Computing Reference Architecture and Taxonomy Working Group as described in Chapter 3 as the framework of reference to identify these gaps in need of standardization. Secondly, we use a broad set of USG business use cases as described in previous sections and from the NIST Cloud Computing Target Business Use Case Working Group, to identify priorities of standardization that will maximize the benefits and meet the more urgent needs of federal government consumers.

9.1 AREAS OF STANDARDIZATION GAPS

As the cloud computing conceptual model indicates, cloud computing consumers do not have direct visibility into the physical computing resources. Instead, consumers interact with service providers through three service model interfaces, IaaS, PaaS, and SaaS, to gain a view of the abstracted computing resource they are using. As described in Chapter 5, *Cloud Computing Standards,* these interaction interfaces can be categorized into two types: (1) functional interfaces that expose the primary function of the service, and (2) management interfaces that let the consumers manage the rented computing resources. The following areas of standardization gaps are observed through the standards inventory.

9.1.1 SAAS FUNCTIONAL INTERFACES

The varieties of the SaaS applications determine what can be consumed by the SaaS consumer. There are varying degrees of functional standardization. SaaS applications are mainly available by using a web browser, and some are consumed as a web service using other application clients, such as standalone desktop applications and mobile applications. Even as most SaaS applications are using web and web service standards to deliver these application capabilities, application-specific data and metadata standards remain standardization gaps in portability and interoperability. For example, email and office productivity application data format standards and interfaces are required to achieve interoperability and portability for migrating from existing systems to cloud systems.

Another important area for standardization is the metadata format and interfaces, in particular, to support compliance needs. For example, standard metadata format and APIs to describe and generate e-discovery metadata for emails, document management systems, financial account systems, etc., will help government consumers to leverage commercial off-the-shelf (COTS) and government off-the-shelf (GOTS) software products to meet e-discovery requirements. This is especially important when email messaging systems, content management systems, or Enterprise Resource Planning (ERP) financial systems migrate to a SaaS model.

9.1.2 SAAS SELF-SERVICE MANAGEMENT INTERFACES

Due to the diverse domain and functional differences among SaaS offerings, the management interfaces used for the consumers to administer and customize the application functionalities are also very diverse. However, certain management functionalities are common, such as those related to user account and credential management. These common management functionalities represent candidates for interoperability standardization.

9.1.3 PAAS FUNCTIONAL INTERFACES

PaaS functional interfaces encompass the runtime environment with supporting libraries and system components for developers to develop and deploy SaaS applications. Standard-based APIs are often part of a PaaS offering such that the PaaS provider can enable existing development for a cloud-based hosting system. However, data format for backup and migration of application workload, including database serialization/de-serialization, need further standardization to support portability.

9.1.4 BUSINESS SUPPORT, PROVISIONING AND CONFIGURATION

In cloud service management areas, the importance of standard data formats and interfaces to describe service-level agreement (SLA) and quality of service (QoS) in traditional IT systems is high. While standards do exist for SLA negotiation and automated service condition matching, the application of these to the fine level of detail expected for large-scale cloud use cases is just developing. Computing resource description and discovery are also in need of standardization as consumers transition from buying and managing resources to renting resources in a cloud system.

This is limited not only to raw computing resources such as virtualized processing, storage, and networking resources, but also includes higher-level abstractions of application processing resources. A standardization gap identified in a related area is metering and billing of service consumptions; data formats and management interfaces are used to report, deliver, and communicate this usage information.

9.1.5 SECURITY

As cloud systems are typically external components in a consumer organization's overall IT system, especially in the outsourced (off-site) deployment models, the need to have seamless security integration calls for interoperable standard interfaces for authentication, authorization, and communication protections. The challenges of identity and access management across different network and administration domains are more prominent in the cloud system as the implementation of these capabilities within the cloud systems are often not the same organization as consumer organization where the identity information originates. Standardization in areas such as identity provisioning, management, secure and efficient replication across different systems, and identity federation will greatly help to improve the identity management capabilities in cloud systems. A related area with specifically wide government usage that can benefit from standardization is single sign-on interface and protocols that support strong authentication.

Government IT systems have strong auditing and compliance needs. In many cases, these requirements must be in place before a system can be approved for operation. The standardization gap in this area exacerbates as the consumer organizations typically do not own or control the underlying system resources that implement the system capabilities. Standardization in policies, processes, and technical controls that support the security auditing requirements, regulations, and law compliance needs to consider the collaboration process between the cloud consumers and providers, their roles, and the sharing of the responsibilities in implementing the system capabilities.

9.1.6 ACCESSIBILITY

A standardized "framework" for exchanging an individual's accessibility requirements does not presently exist. A standardized method for automatic recognition of a user's requirements for accessibility would automatically identify the need for having an accessibility requirement known after the first request, for example, captioning for all subsequent video. (Note: Such automatic recognition features can trigger privacy issues depending how the information is used.)

9.2 STANDARDIZATION PRIORITIES BASED ON USG CLOUD COMPUTING ADOPTION PRIORITIES

As described in the Federal Cloud Computing Strategy, some cloud computing business use cases have higher priorities than others. The requirements expressed in these high-priority target business use cases can be used to prioritize the standardization gaps. For example, various USG groups have identified data center consolidation using virtualization technologies as one of the primary goals in the next few years. Migrating collaboration applications, including email messaging (email, contacts, and calendars) and online office productivity application, to the cloud system is also quoted as an early target of government cloud operation.

By analyzing the USG cloud computing target business use cases with their specific technical requirements, one can point out the following basic drivers that can be used to prioritize cloud computing standard gaps:

- The focus on supporting migration of system workload, including data, metadata and processing logic of existing in-house IT systems, to cloud-based systems to ensure continuous operation; this focus is centered on portability standards.

- The need to have interoperability between existing in-house IT systems and cloud-based systems, as cloud-deployed systems will be only a part of the overall enterprise system; this need is centered on interoperability standards, including security standards.

- The need to help government consumers to choose and buy the most cost-effective solutions. If a cloud solution is not as economical as an in-house traditional IT system, there is no financial incentive to move the system to the cloud system.

Based on these understandings, the following areas of standardization gaps in cloud computing are of higher priority for USG cloud consumers:

9.2.1 SECURITY AUDITING AND COMPLIANCE

Data format standards for auditing, compliance data and metadata are needed. Standard interfaces to retrieve and manage these data and metadata assets are also required to be integrated with existing tools and processes. In addition, policy, process and technical control standards are needed to support more manageable assessment and accreditation processes, which are often a prerequisite before a system is put in operation.

9.2.2 IDENTITY AND ACCESS MANAGEMENT

As described earlier, security integration of a cloud system into existing enterprise security infrastructure is a must for the majority of government systems with moderate and greater impact. Existing practices of external cloud-based components in identity and access management is often based on proprietary and custom integration solutions. Constant and standard ways of provisioning identity data, managing identity data, and replicating to-and-from cloud system components, are needed to ensure that consumer organizations' short-term and long-terms needs are met.

Many government systems are required to have strong authentication, such as two-factor authentication implemented in an Internet-deployed system. Standards in supporting single sign-on and strong authentication are a must for these types of systems.

9.2.3 SAAS APPLICATION SPECIFIC DATA AND METADATA

To support the urgent need to migrate certain applications to the cloud system, application-specific data and metadata format standards are required. This is an area where a lot of SaaS providers currently help consumer organizations to migrate their existing system by offering custom conversion and migration support. However, without standards in data and metadata format for these applications, the potential danger exists of creating non-interoperable islands of cloud solutions and vendor lock-in. For example, some SaaS email solutions may not be fully interoperable with in-house email and calendaring solutions. There are specific email working groups[25] in the federal cloud computing initiative that are looking into putting forward specific metadata standardization requirements for email security, privacy, and record management. Other SaaS functional areas, such as document management and financial systems, are also among the high-priority areas where standards in data and metadata are needed.

9.2.4 RESOURCE DESCRIPTION AND DISCOVERY

Description and discovery of computing resources needs are usually the first steps for consumers to take to start using cloud computing. Standard methods to describe resources will facilitate programmatically interoperable cloud applications to discover and use cloud computing resources such as computing resources, storage resources, or application resources. To establish private or community cloud computing as a way to implement data center consolidation, standards for these areas are important to avoid the implementation of vendor-specific interfaces, and also helps to increase the dynamic provisioning capabilities of the solution and utility of the computing resources.

---

[25] https://www.fbo.gov/utils/view?id=4c4e37f4f1bcd2cb8d0a16f0e1b0ddbe

The following table summarizes the areas of standardization gaps and standardization priorities based on USG cloud computing adoption requirements.

9.2.5 SUMMARY OF STANDARDIZATION GAPS AND STANDARDIZATION PRIORITIES

Table 17 – Areas of Standardization Gaps and Standardization Priorities provides a mapping of present standards gaps and how they relate to USG high priorities.

Area of Standardization Gaps	High Priorities for Standardization Based On USG Requirements
SaaS Functional Interfaces (9.1.1 / page 70), e.g., - Data format and interface standards for email and office productivity - Metadata format and interface standards for e-discovery	High standardization priorities on: - SaaS application specific data and metadata format standards to support interoperability and portability requirement when migrating high-value, low-risk applications to SaaS (Section 9.2.3).
SaaS Self-Service Management Interfaces (Section 9.1.2), e.g., - Interface standards related to user account and credential management	Not a high standardization priority at this time
PaaS Functional Interfaces (Section 9.1.3), e.g., - Standards of data format to support database serialization and de-serialization	Not a high standardization priority at this time
Business Support, Provisioning and Configuration (Section 9.1.4), e.g., - Standards for describing cloud service-level agreement and quality of services - Standards for describing and discovering cloud service resources - Standards for metering and billing of service consumptions and usage	High standardization priorities on: - Resource description and discovery standards to support data center consolidation using private and community IaaS cloud systems (Section 9.2.4)

Area of Standardization Gaps	High Priorities for Standardization Based On USG Requirements
Security (Section 9.1.5), e.g., - Standards for identity provisioning and management across different network and administration domains - Standards for secure and efficient replication of identity and access policy information across systems - Single Sign-On interface and protocol standards that support strong authentication - Standards in policies, processes, and technical controls in supporting the security auditing, regulation, and law compliance needs	High standardization priorities on: - Security auditing and compliance standards to support secure deployment, assess, and accreditation process for cloud-specific deployment (Section 9.2.1) - Identity and access management standards to support secure integration of cloud systems into existing enterprise security infrastructure (Section 9.2.2)
Accessibility (Section 9.1.6), e.g. - Standardized "framework" for exchanging an individual's accessibility requirements	Not a high standardization priority at this time

Table 17 – Areas of Standardization Gaps and Standardization Priorities

10 CONCLUSIONS AND RECOMMENDATIONS

10.1 CONCLUSIONS

Cloud computing can enable USG agencies to achieve cost savings and increased ability to quickly create and deploy enterprise applications. While cloud computing technology challenges many traditional approaches to data center and enterprise application design and management, requirements for accessibility, interoperability, performance, portability, and security remain critically important for successful deployments. Technically sound and timely standards are instrumental to ensuring that requirements for interoperability, portability, and security are met.

There is a fast-changing landscape of cloud computing-relevant standardization under way in a number of SDOs. While there are only a few approved cloud computing-specific standards at present, USG agencies should be encouraged to participate in specific cloud computing standards development projects that support their priorities in cloud computing services.

10.2 RECOMMEDATION TO USG AGENCIES TO HELP ACCELERATE THE DEVELOPMENT AND USE OF CLOUD COMPUTING STANDARDS

USG laws and policies encourage federal agency participation in the development and use of voluntary consensus standards and in conformity assessment activities. The following recommendations provide further guidance on how agencies can help to accelerate the development and use of cloud computing standards.

Recommendation 1 – Contribute Agency Requirements

Agencies should coordinate and contribute clear and comprehensive user requirements for cloud computing standards projects.

Recommendation 2 – Participate in Standards Development

Agencies should actively participate and coordinate in cloud computing standards development projects that are of high priority to their agency missions. The January 17, 2012, White House Memorandum, M-12-08, lists five fundamental strategic objectives for federal government agencies whenever engaging in standards development:

- Produce timely, effective standards and efficient conformity assessment schemes that are essential to addressing an identified need;
- Achieve cost-efficient, timely, and effective solutions to legitimate regulatory, procurement, and policy objectives;

- Promote standards and standardization systems that promote and sustain innovation and foster competition;

- Enhance U.S. growth and competitiveness and ensure non-discrimination, consistent with international obligations; and

- Facilitate international trade and avoid the creation of unnecessary obstacles to trade.

Recommendation 3 – Encourage Testing to Accelerate Technically Sound Standards-Based Deployments

Agencies should support the concurrent development of conformity and interoperability assessment schemes to accelerate the development and use of technically sound cloud computing standards and standards-based products, processes, and services. Agencies should also include consideration of conformity assessment approaches currently in place that take account of elements from international systems, to minimize duplicative testing and encourage private sector support.

Recommendation 4 – Specify Cloud Computing Standards

Agencies should specify cloud computing standards in their procurements and grant guidance when multiple vendors offer standards-based implementations and there is evidence of successful interoperability testing.

Recommendation 5 – USG-Wide Use of Cloud Computing Standards

To support USG requirements for accessibility, interoperability, performance, portability, and security in cloud computing, the Federal Cloud Computing Standards and Technology Working Group, in coordination with the Federal CIO Council Cloud Computing Executive Steering Committee (CCESC) and the Cloud First Task Force, should recommend specific cloud computing standards and best practices for USG-wide use.

11 BIBLIOGRAPHY

This section provides sources for additional information.

Distributed Management Task Force (DMTF)

- Interoperable Clouds White Paper

DSP-IS0101 Cloud Interoperability White Paper V1.0.0

This white paper describes a snapshot of the work being done in the DMTF Open Cloud Standards Incubator, including use cases and reference architecture as they relate to the interfaces between a cloud service provider and a cloud service consumer.
http://dmtf.org/sites/default/files/standards/documents/DSP-IS0101_1.0.0.pdf

- Architecture for Managing Clouds White Paper

DSP-IS0102 Architecture for Managing Clouds White Paper V1.0.0

This white paper is one of two Phase 2 deliverables from the DMTF Cloud Incubator and describes the reference architecture as it relates to the interfaces between a cloud service provider and a cloud service consumer. The goal of the Incubator is to define a set of architectural semantics that unify the interoperable management of enterprise and cloud computing.
http://dmtf.org/sites/default/files/standards/documents/DSP-IS0102_1.0.0.pdf

- Use Cases and Interactions for Managing Clouds White Paper

DSP-IS0103 Use Cases and Interactions for Managing Clouds White Paper V1.0.0

This document is one of two documents that together describe how standardized interfaces and data formats can be used to manage clouds. The document focuses on use cases, interactions, and data formats. http://dmtf.org/sites/default/files/standards/documents/DSP-IS0103_1.0.0.pdf

Global Inter-Cloud Technology Forum (GICTF)

Use Cases and Functional Requirements for Inter-Cloud Computing
Published on August 2010
http://www.gictf.jp/doc/GICTF_Whitepaper_20100809.pdf

This white paper describes three areas of advantages of inter-cloud computing, which are assured or prioritized performance, availability, and convenience of combined services. Several use cases of inter-cloud computing are provided with details according to these three areas, such as assured performance against transient overload, disaster recovery and service continuity for availability, and federated service provisions, followed by sequential procedures and functional requirements for each use case. Essential functional entities and interfaces are identified to meet these described requirements.

Technical Requirements for Supporting the Intercloud Networking
Published on April 2012
http://www.gictf.jp/doc/GICTF_NWSWG-WhitePaper_e_20120420.pdf

Based on the preceding Inter-Cloud use cases and functional requirements, this white paper describes technical requirements for each use case such as assured service level, disaster recovery, service continuity, and federated service provisions.

It also shows expected technical evolutions in a next few years.

TM Forum

Cloud Monetization Differentiating Cloud Services
Released: January 2012
https://www.tmforum.org/WhitePapers/CloudMonetization/47730/article.html

This whitepaper explores the various cloud bill requirements and complexities for the different cloud business models. It will also explore the expectations from customers of cloud services, with respect to billing for cloud services, highlighting gaps and potential risks to service provider success, as well as recommend areas for further action.

12 APPENDIX A – NIST FEDERAL INFORMATION PROCESSING STANDARDS AND SPECIAL PUBLICATIONS RELEVANT TO CLOUD COMPUTING

Federal Information Process Standards Publication (FIPS) 199, *Standards for Security Categorization of Federal Information and Information Systems*

Federal Information Processing Standards Publication (FIPS) 200, *Minimum Security Requirements for Federal Information and Information Systems*

NIST Special Publication 500-292, *NIST Cloud Computing Reference Architecture, September 2011*

NIST Special Publication 500-293, *U.S. Government Cloud Computing Technology Roadmap, Release 1.0 (Draft), Volume I High-Priority Requirements to Further USG Agency Cloud Computing Adoption, November 2011*

NIST Special Publication 500-293, *U.S. Government Cloud Computing Technology Roadmap, Release 1.0 (Draft), Volume II Useful Information for Cloud Adopters*, November 2011

NIST Special Publication 800-37 Rev 1, *Guide for Applying the Risk Management Framework to Federal Information Systems: A Security Life Cycle Approach*

NIST Special Publication 800-53 Rev 4, *Security and Privacy Controls for Federal Information Systems and Organizations*

NIST Special Publication 800-53 Rev 3, *Recommended Security Controls for Federal Information Systems and Organizations*

NIST Special Publication 800-92, *Guide to Computer Security Log Management*

NIST Special Publication 800-125, *Guide to Security for Full Virtualization Technologies*

NIST Special Publication 800-137, *Information Security Continuous Monitoring for Federal Information Systems and Organizations*

NIST Special Publication 800-144, *Guidelines on Security and Privacy Issues in Public Cloud Computing*

NIST Special Publication 800-145, *The NIST Definition of Cloud Computing*

NIST Special Publication 800-146, *Cloud Computing Synopsis and Recommendations*

13 APPENDIX B – DEFINITIONS

Accreditation - Third-party attestation related to a conformity assessment body conveying formal demonstration of its competence to carry out specific conformity assessment tasks [SOURCE: ISO/IEC 17000:2004, Conformity assessment — Vocabulary and general principles]

Accessibility
– Measurable characteristics that indicate the degree to which a system is available to, and usable by, individuals with disabilities. The most common disabilities include those associated with vision, hearing, and mobility, as well as cognitive disabilities.
[SOURCE: This report]

– Usability of a product, service, environment or facility by individuals with the widest range of capabilities
NOTE 1 issues.
Although "accessibility" typically addresses users who have a disability, the concept is not limited to disability.
NOTE 2 Adapted from ISO/TS 16071:2003, Ergonomics of human-system interaction -- Guidance on accessibility for human-computer interfaces
[SOURCE: ISO/IEC 24751-1:2008, Information technology -- Individualized adaptability and accessibility in e-learning, education and training -- Part 1: Framework and reference model]

Attestation – Issue of a statement, based on a decision following review that fulfillment of specified requirements has been demonstrated
[SOURCE: ISO/IEC 17000:2004, Conformity assessment — Vocabulary and general principles]

Certification – Third-party attestation related to products, processes, systems or persons.
NOTE 1 Certification of a management system is sometimes also called registration.
NOTE 2 Certification is applicable to all objects of conformity assessment except for conformity assessment bodies themselves, to which accreditation is applicable.
[SOURCE: ISO/IEC 17000:2004, Conformity assessment — Vocabulary and general principles]

Conformity assessment – Demonstration that specified requirements relating to a product process, system, person or body are fulfilled [ISO/IEC 17000:2004, Conformity assessment — Vocabulary and general principles]
[SOURCE: Guidance on Federal Conformity Assessment Activities
http://gsi.nist.gov/global/index.cfm/L1-5/L2-45/A-332]
[SOURCE: The ABC's of the U.S. Conformity Assessment System
http://gsi.nist.gov/global/index.cfm/L1-5/L2-45/A-337]

First-party conformity assessment activity – Conformity assessment activity that is performed by the person or organization that provides the object
NOTE: The first-, second- and third-party descriptors used to characterize conformity assessment activities with respect to a given object are not to be confused with the legal identification of the relevant parties to a contract.
[SOURCE: ISO/IEC 17000:2004, Conformity assessment — Vocabulary and general principles]

Data Migration – The periodic transfer of data from one hardware or software configuration to another or from one generation of computer technology to a subsequent generation. Migration is a necessary action for retaining the integrity of the data and for allowing users to search, retrieve, and make use of data in the face of constantly changing technology.
[SOURCE : http://www.ischool.utexas.edu/~scisco/lis389c.5/email/gloss.html]

Information Technologies (IT) – Encompasses all technologies for the capture, storage, retrieval, processing, display, representation, organization, management, security, transfer, and interchange of data and information.
[SOURCE: This report]

Interoperability – The capabilities to communicate, execute programs, or transfer data among various functional units under specified conditions.
[SOURCE: American National Standard Dictionary of Information Technology (ANSDIT)]

Maintainability – A measure of the ease with which maintenance of a functional unit can be performed using prescribed procedures and resources. Synonymous with serviceability. [SOURCE: American National Standard Dictionary of Information Technology (ANSDIT)]

Network Resilience – A computing infrastructure that provides continuous business operation (i.e., highly resistant to disruption and able to operate in a degraded mode if damaged), rapid recovery if failure does occur, and the ability to scale to meet rapid or unpredictable demands.
[SOURCE: The Committee on National Security Systems Instruction No 4009,"National Information Assurance Glossary." CNSSI-4009]

Performance – The ability to track service and resource usage levels and to provide feedback on the responsiveness and reliability of the network.
[SOURCE: ETSI and 3GPP Dictionary]

Portability – The capability of a program to be executed on various types of data processing systems with little or no modification and without converting the program to a different language.
[SOURCE: American National Standard Dictionary of Information Technology (ANSDIT)]

- 1) The ability to transfer data from one system to another without being required to recreate or reenter data descriptions or to modify significantly the application being transported.
- 2) The ability of software or of a system to run on more than one type or size of computer under more than one operating system.

[SOURCE: Federal Standard 1037C, Glossary of Telecommunication Terms, 1996]

Privacy – Information privacy is the assured, proper, and consistent collection, processing, communication, use, and disposition of personal information (PI) and personally identifiable information (PII) throughout its life cycle.
[SOURCE: NIST Cloud Computing Reference Architecture and Taxonomy Working Group]

Reference implementation – An implementation of a standard to be used as a definitive interpretation for the requirements in that standard. Reference implementations can serve many purposes. They can be used to verify that the standard is implementable, validate conformance test tools, and support interoperability testing among other implementations. A reference implementation may or may not have the quality of a commercial product or service that implements the standard.
[SOURCE: This report]

Reliability – A measure of the ability of a functional unit to perform a required function under given conditions for a given time interval.
[SOURCE: American National Standard Dictionary of Information Technology (ANSDIT)]
A time server / time service provides accurate and **reliable** network time where various vendor's products are calibrated to NIST's Time Server / Time Service, for example in wide area computing **TIME** sharing, metrics and metering of computational node, cloud center traversals using industry standard groups protocols such as IEEE C37.118, IEC 61850, and IEEE 802.1AG for execution management, governance of execution run time where a reference time stamp marks the scheduling, e.g., start, stop and time to live of a run time service or distributed algorithm.

Resilience

– The ability to reduce the magnitude and/or duration of disruptive events to critical infrastructure. The effectiveness of a resilient infrastructure or enterprise depends upon its ability to anticipate, absorb, adapt to, and/or rapidly recover from a potentially disruptive event. [SOURCE: Critical Infrastructure Resilience Final Report and Recommendations, National Infrastructure Advisory Council, September 8, 2009]

– The adaptive capability of an organization in a complex and changing environment.
[SOURCE: **ASIS** International, ASIS SPC.1-2009, American National Standard, Organizational Resilience: Security, Preparedness, and Continuity Management System – Requirements with Guidance for Use.]

Risk Management – Coordinated activities to direct and control an organization with regard to risk ISO/IEC 27005, Information Technology – Security Techniques – Information Security Risk Management

Second-party conformity assessment activity – Conformity assessment activity that is performed by a person or organization that has a user interest in the object
[ISO/IEC 17000:2004, Conformity assessment — Vocabulary and general principles]

Security – Refers to information security. Information security means protecting information and information systems from unauthorized access, use, disclosure, disruption, modification, or destruction in order to provide:

- Integrity, which means guarding against improper information modification or destruction, and includes ensuring information non-repudiation and authenticity;
- Confidentiality, which means preserving authorized restrictions on access and disclosure, including means for protecting personal privacy and proprietary information; and
- Availability, which means ensuring timely and reliable access to and use of information.

[SOURCE: ~~Title III of the E-Government Act, entitled the Federal Information Security Management Act of 2002 (FISMA)~~]

Standard

– A document, established by consensus and approved by a recognized body that provides for common and repeated use, rules, guidelines or characteristics for activities or their results, aimed at the achievement of the optimum degree of order in a given context. Note: Standards should be based on the consolidated results of science, technology, and experience, and aimed at the promotion of optimum community benefits.
[SOURCE: ISO/IEC Guide 2:2004, Standardization and related activities – General Vocabulary, definition 3.2]

– A document that may provide the requirements for: a product, process or service; a management or engineering process; or a testing methodology. An example of a product standard is the multipart ISO/IEC 24727, *Integrated circuit card programming interfaces*. An example of a management process standard is the ISO/IEC 27000, *Information security management systems*, family of standards. An example of an engineering process standard is ISO/IEC 15288, System life cycle processes. An example of a testing methodology standard is the multipart ISO/IEC 19795, *Biometric Performance Testing and Reporting*.

Standards Developing Organization (SDO) – Any organization that develops and approves standards using various methods to establish consensus among its participants. Such organizations may be: accredited, such as ANSI-accredited IEEE; or international treaty-based, such as the ITU-T; or international private sector-based, such as ISO/IEC; or an international consortium, such as OASIS or IETF; or a government agency.
SOURCE: [This report]

Third-party conformity assessment activity – Conformity assessment activity that is performed by a person or body that is independent of the person or organization that provides the object and user interests in that object
[SOURCE: ISO/IEC 17000:2004, Conformity assessment — Vocabulary and general principles]

Test – Technical operation that consists of the determination of one or more characteristics of a given product, process or service according to a specified procedure. [ISO/IEC Guide 2:2004]

Testing – Action of carrying out one or more tests. [ISO/IEC Guide 2:2004]

Usability – The extent to which a product can be used by specified users to achieve specified goals with effectiveness, efficiency, and satisfaction in a specified context of use.
[SOURCE: ISO 9241-11:1998 Ergonomic requirements for office work with visual display terminals (VDTs) – Part 11: Guidance on usability and ISO/IEC 25062:2006 Software engineering – Software product Quality Requirements and Evaluation (SquaRE) – Common Industry Format (CIF) for usability test reports]

14 APPENDIX C – ACRONYMS

ANSDIT	American National Standard Dictionary of Information Technology
API	Application Programming Interface
BOD	Business Object Document
CCESC	Cloud Computing Executive Steering Committee
CDMI	Cloud Data Management Interface
CDN	Content Delivery Network
CIMI	Cloud Infrastructure Management Interface
CIO	Chief Information Officer
CMWG	Cloud Management Working Group
COTS	Commercial off-the-shelf
CPU	Central Processing Unit
CRM	Customer Relationship Management
CRUD	Create-Read-Update-Delete
CSA	Cloud Security Alliance
CSIRT	Computer Security Incident Response Teams
CSW	Catalog Service for the Web
DCIFed	DCI Federation Working Group
DISR	Defense IT Standards Registry
DMTF	Distributed Management Task Force
DoD	Department of Defense (USA)
ebRIM	Electronic business Registry Information Model
ebXML	Electronic Business using eXtensible Markup Language
ERP	Enterprise Resource Planning
EULA	End User License Agreement
FCCI	Federal Cloud Computing Initiative
FEA	Federal Enterprise Architecture
FIPS	Federal Information Processing Standards
GEIA	Government Electronics & Information Technology Association
GICTF	Global Inter-Cloud Technology Forum
GLUE	Grid Laboratory Uniform Environment
GOTS	Government off-the-shelf
HTML	HyperText Markup Language
HTTP	Hypertext Transfer Protocol
ID-WSF	IDentity Web Service Framework
I/O	Input/Output
IaaS	Infrastructure as a Service

IEC	International Electrotechnical Commission
IEEE	Institute of Electrical and Electronic Engineers
IETF	Internet Engineering Task Force
IODEF	Incident Object Description Format
IP	Internet Protocol
ISIMC	Information Security and Identity Management Committee
ISO	International Organization for Standardization
ISO/IEC JTC 1	International Organization for Standardization/International Electrotechnical Commission Joint Technical Committee 1 Information Technology
IT (ICT)	Information Technology (Note: it is often referred to as ICT [Information and Communications Technologies])
ITU	International Telecommunication Union (The)
ITU-T	ITU Telecommunication Standardization Sector
J2EE	Java 2 Platform, Enterprise Edition
JSON	JavaScript Object Notation
KMIP	Key Management Interoperability Protocol
LDAP	Lightweight Directory Access Protocol
MID	Mobile Internet Devices (USA)
MIL-STDS	Military Standards (USA)
NIEM	National Information Exchange Model
NIST	National Institute of Standards and Technology
NIST SP	NIST Special Publication
OAGi	Open Applications Group
OAGIS	Open Applications Group Integration Specification
OASIS	Organization for the Advancement of Structured Information Standards
OAuth	Open Authorization Protocol
OCC	Open Cloud Consortium
OCCI	Open Cloud Computing Interface
ODF	Open Document Format
OGC	Open Geospatial Consortium
OGF	Open Grid Forum
OGSA	Open Grid Services Architecture
OMG	Object Management Group
OOXML	Office Open XML
OS	Operating System
OVF	Open Virtualization Format

P2P	Peer-to-Peer
PaaS	Platform as a Service
PDA	Personal Digital Assistant
PHP	PHP: Hypertext Preprocessor
PI	Personal Information
PII	Personal Identifiable Information
PIV	Personal Identity Verification
PKI	Public Key Infrastructure
QoS	Quality of Service
RDF	Resource Description Framework
REST	Representational State Transfer
RSS	Really Simple Syndication
SaaS	Software as a Service
SAJACC	Standards Acceleration to Jumpstart Adoption of Cloud Computing
SAML	Security Assertion Markup Language
SCAP	Security Content Automation Protocol
SDOs	Standards Developing Organizations
SLA	Service Level Agreement
SNIA	Storage Networking Industry Association
SOA	Service-Oriented Architecture
SOAP	Simple Object Access Protocol
SPML	Service Provisioning Markup Language
SSL	Secure Sockets Layer
SSO	Standard Setting Organization
STANAGS	Standardization Agreements
TCG	Trusted Computing Group
TCP	Transmission Control Protocol
TLS	Transport Layer Security
UDDI	Universal Description Discovery and Integration
USG	United States Government
VM	Virtual Machine
W3C	World Wide Web Consortium
WG	Working Group
XACML	OASIS eXtensible Access Control Markup Language
XML	Extensible Markup Language

15 APPENDIX D – STANDARDS DEVELOPING ORGANIZATIONS

Global Information and Communications Technologies (IT) standards are developed in many venues. Such standards are created through collaborative efforts that have a global reach, are voluntary, and are widely adopted by the marketplace across national borders. These standards are developed not only by national member-based international standards bodies, but also by consortia groups and other organizations.

In July 2009, a Wiki site for cloud computing standards coordination was established: cloud-standards.org. The goal of the site is to document the activities of the various SDOs working on cloud computing standards.

The following is a list of SDOs that have standards projects and standards relevant to cloud computing.

ATIS

ATIS is accredited by the American National Standards Institute (ANSI). ATIS is the North American Organizational Partner for the 3rd Generation Partnership Project (3GPP), a founding Partner of oneM2M, a member and major U.S. contributor to the International Telecommunication Union (ITU) Radio and Telecommunications sectors, and a member of the Inter-American Telecommunication Commission (CITEL).

The ATIS Cloud Services Forum (CSF) facilitates the adoption and advancement of cloud services from a network and IT perspective. Drawing upon business use cases that leverage cloud services' potential, the Forum addresses industry priorities and develops implementable solutions for this evolving marketplace. CSF is working to ensure that cloud services – as offered by service providers – are quickly operationalized to facilitate the delivery of interoperable, secure, and managed services. Current priorities include inter-carrier telepresence, content distribution network interconnection, cloud services framework, virtual desktop, virtual private network, and development of a cloud services checklist for onboarding.

CloudAudit

CloudAudit (A6), a working group under the auspices of the CSA (Cloud Security Alliance). Founded in January 2010, *CloudAudit* aims to enable cloud service providers to offer their clients some degree of transparency in an automated, programmatic manner. The group addresses the challenges of lack of transparency and audit requirements in a cloud-based system. The official objective of this working group is to develop a common interface for the automation of the Audit, Assertion, Assessment and Assurance of IaaS (infrastructure as a service), PaaS (platform as a service) and SaaS (software as a service) environments. As of October 2010, *CloudAudit* is officially under the auspices of the Cloud Security Alliance.

Distributed Management Task Force (DMTF)

DMTF spans the industry with 160 member companies and organizations, and more than 4,000 active participants crossing 43 countries. DMTF members collaborate to develop IT management standards that promote multi-vendor interoperability worldwide.

Open Virtualization Format (OVF)
Open Virtualization Format (OVF) V1.0
OVF 1.1 has been designated as ANSI INCITS 469 2010, and ISO/IEC 17203: 2011.
Open Virtualization Format (OVF), OVF 2.0

This specification describes an open, secure, portable, efficient, and extensible format for the packaging and distribution of software to be run in virtual machines. OVF 2.0 includes support for network configuration along with the ability to encrypt the package to ensure safe delivery.

Open Virtualization Format (OVF)
DSP0243 Open Virtualization Format (OVF) V1.1.0
OVF has been designated as ANSI INCITS 469 2010, ISO/IEC 17203:2011.
This specification describes an open, secure, portable, efficient, and extensible format for the packaging and distribution of software to be run in virtual machines.

Open Cloud Standards Incubator
DMTF's Open Cloud Standards Incubator focused on standardizing interactions between cloud systems by developing cloud management use cases, architectures, and interactions. This work was completed in July 2010. The work has now transitioned to the Cloud Management Working Group.

Cloud Management Working Group (CMWG)
The CMWG will develop a set of prescriptive specifications that deliver architectural semantics as well as implementation details to achieve interoperable management of clouds between service requestors/developers and providers. This WG will propose a resource model that, at a minimum, captures the key artifacts identified in the use cases and interactions for managing clouds document produced by the Open Cloud Incubator. This group has developed and released the Cloud Infrastructure Management Inter Face (CIMI).

Using the recommendations developed by DMTF's Open Cloud Standards Incubator, the Cloud Management Workgroup (CMWG) is focused on standardizing interactions between cloud systems by developing specifications that deliver architectural semantics and implementation details to achieve interoperable cloud management between service providers and their consumers and developers.

Institute of Electrical and Electronic Engineers (IEEE)

The IEEE Standards Association (IEEE-SA), a globally recognized standards-setting body within the IEEE, develops consensus standards through an open process that engages industry and brings together a broad stakeholder community. IEEE standards set specifications and best practices based on current scientific and technological knowledge. The IEEE-SA has a portfolio of over 900 active standards and more than 500 standards under development.

The IEEE P2301 Working Group (Cloud Profiles) is developing the Guide for Cloud Portability and Interoperability Profiles (CPIP). The guide advises cloud computing ecosystem participants (cloud vendors, service providers, and users) of standards-based choices in areas such as application interfaces, portability interfaces, management interfaces, interoperability interfaces, file formats, and operation conventions.

The EEE P2302 Working Group (Intercloud) is developing the Standard for Intercloud Interoperability and Federation (SIIF). This standard defines topology, functions, and governance for cloud-to-cloud interoperability and federation.

The Internet Engineering Task Force (IETF)

The Internet Engineering Task Force (IETF) issues the standards and protocols used to protect the Internet and enable global electronic commerce. The IETF develops cyber security standards for the Internet. Current activities include Public Key Infrastructure Using X.509 (PKIX), Internet Protocol Security (IPsec), Transport Layer Security (TLS), Secure Electronic Mail (S/MIME V3), DNS Security Extensions (DNSSEC), and Keying and Authentication for Routing Protocols (karp). Another IETF standard is the Incident Object Description Format (IODEF), which provides a framework for sharing information commonly exchanged by Computer Security Incident Response Teams (CSIRTs) about computer security incidents. IODEF is an underpinning for the National Information Exchange Model (NIEM), which enables jurisdictions to effectively share critical information on cyber incident management, security configuration management, security vulnerability management, etc.

International Organization for Standardization/International Electrotechnical Commission Joint Technical Committee 1 Information Technology (ISO/IEC JTC 1)

ISO/IEC JTC 1 is the standards development environment where experts come together to develop worldwide Information and Communication Technology (ICT) standards for business and consumer applications. Additionally, JTC 1 provides the standards approval environment for integrating diverse and complex ICT technologies. These standards rely upon the core infrastructure technologies developed by JTC 1 centers of expertise complemented by specifications developed in other organizations. Presently, there are 91 country members. Approximately 2100 technical experts from around the world work within JTC 1. There are presently 18 JTC 1 Subcommittees (SCs) in which most of JTC 1 standards projects are being developed.

JTC 1 SC 27 (IT Security Techniques) is the one JTC 1 SC that is completely focused on cyber security standardization. There are currently three cloud security standards projects in SC27.

ISO/IEC 4th WD 27017, Information security management - Guidelines on information security controls for the use of cloud computing services based on ISO/IEC 27002 (Technical Specification)
Provides organizations using or expecting to use cloud computing services with guidelines for initiating, implementing, maintaining, and improving the information security management based upon ISO/IEC 27002:2005 specific to the cloud computing services.

ISO/IEC 2nd WD 27018, Code of practice for data protection controls for public cloud computing services
Establishes commonly accepted data protection control objectives, controls, and guidelines for implementing controls to meet the requirements identified by a risk assessment. Applies primarily to organizations providing cloud computing services that act as PII processors.

ISO/IEC 1st WD 27036-4, Information technology – Security techniques – Information security for supplier relationships – Part 4: Guidelines for security of cloud services
Provides cloud service acquirers and suppliers with guidance on: managing the information security risks caused by using cloud services; integrating information security processes and practices into the cloud –based product and service life cycle processes, while supporting information security controls; responding to risks specific to the acquisition or provision of cloud-based services that can have an information security impact on organisations using these services.

In October 2009, JTC 1 established a new Subcommittee, JTC 1 SC 38 Distributed application platforms and services (DAPS). JTC 1 SC 38 has subsequently established Working Group 3, Cloud computing.

Two Collaborative Teams have been established by ISO/IEC JTC1/SC38/WG3 and ITU-T SG13/WP6:

- Collaborative Team on Cloud Computing Overview and Vocabulary (CT-CCVOCAB)
- Collaborative Team on Cloud Computing Reference Architecture (CT-CCRA).

International Telecommunication Union (ITU) Telecommunication Standardization Sector (ITU-T)

The ITU-T develops international standards for the telecommunications including voice, data, and video. The primary Study Groups in the ITU-T that are developing standards for cloud computing are SG13: Future networks including cloud computing, mobile and next-generation networks, and SG17: Security.

A new ITU-T Working Party in Study Group 13 (i.e., WP6/13). WP6/13 includes three new Questions or areas of cloud computing study. WP6/13 is currently developing a number of Draft Cloud Computing Recommendation and has established two Collaborative Teams with ISO/IEC JTC 1/SC38. See the JTC 1 SC 38 WG 3 above.

Kantara Initiative

Kantara Initiative was established on April 20, 2009, by leaders of several foundations and associations working on various aspects of digital identity, aka "the Venn of Identity." It is intended to be a robust and well-funded focal point for collaboration to address the issues shared across the identity community: Interoperability and Compliance Testing; Identity Assurance; Policy and Legal Issues; Privacy; Ownership and Liability; UX and Usability; Cross-Community Coordination and Collaboration; Education and Outreach; Market Research; Use Cases and Requirements; Harmonization; and Tool Development.

Kantara Initiative is not a standards setting organization for technical specifications. The output of Kantara Initiative is called a Recommendation. Any kind of work can be done in Kantara Initiative but if the work is a technical specification it must be submitted to a standards setting organization upon completion. Other "standards" work such as Operational Frameworks or Usability Guidelines or Interoperability Testing Procedures are the primary focus of Kantara Initiative and will be both developed and maintained by the organization.

OASIS (Organization for the Advancement of Structured Information Standards)

Founded in 1993, OASIS is a not-for-profit consortium. OASIS develops open standards for the global information society. The consortium produces Eeb services standards along with standards for security, e-business, and standardization efforts in the public sector and for application-specific markets. OASIS has more than 5,000 participants representing over 600 organizations and individual members in 100 countries.

Technical Committees specific to cloud computing include:

~~Cloud Application Management for Platforms (CAMP)~~ – The purpose of this TC is to define models, mechanisms, and protocols for the management of applications in, and their use of, a Platform as a Service (PaaS) environment.

~~Cloud Authorization (CloudAuthZ)~~ – The focus of this TC is to develop an interoperable protocol for PaaS (self-service) management interfaces for cloud users to use in developing, deploying and administration of their applications. PaaS management should allow for, but not require, IaaS management to manage the deployment of resources for an application.

~~Topology and Orchestration Specification for Cloud Applications (TOSCA)~~ – The TC was formed in December, 2011, with the goal to substantially enhance the portability of cloud applications and the IT services that comprise them running on complex virtual and physical software and hardware infrastructure."

The Open Cloud Consortium (OCC)

OCC is a member-driven organization that develops reference implementations, benchmarks, and standards for cloud computing. The OCC operates cloud testbeds, such as the Open Cloud Testbed and the OCC Virtual Network Testbed. The OCC also manages cloud computing infrastructure to support scientific research, such as the Open Science Data Cloud.

Open Grid Forum (OGF)

Open Grid Forum (OGF) is a leading standards developing organization operating in the areas of grid, cloud, and related forms of advanced distributed computing. The OGF community pursues these topics through an open process for development, creation, and promotion of relevant specifications and use cases.

OGF engages partners and participants throughout the international arena to champion architectural blueprints related to cloud and grid computing and the associated specifications to enable the pervasive adoption of advanced distributed computing techniques for business and research worldwide.

Advanced computing built on OGF standards enables organizations to share computing and information resources across department and organizational boundaries in a secure, efficient manner. Organizations throughout the world use production distributed architectures built on these features to collaborate in areas as diverse as scientific research, drug discovery, financial risk analysis, and product design. The capacity and flexibility of distributed computing enables organizations to solve problems that until recently were not feasible to address due to interoperability, portability, security, cost and data-integration constraints.

Cloud systems, grids, and virtualized distributed architectures reduce costs through automation and improved IT resource utilization and improve organizational agility by enabling more efficient business processes. OGF's extensive experience has enabled distributed computing built on these architectures to become a more flexible, efficient, and utility-like global computing infrastructure.

Standardization is the key to realizing the full vision and benefits of distributed computing. The standards developed by OGF enable the diverse resources of today's modern computing environment to be discovered, accessed, allocated, monitored, and managed as interconnected flexible virtual systems, even when provided by different vendors and/or operated by different organizations.

Open Cloud Computing Interface (OCCI) Working Group
The purpose of this group is the creation of a practical solution to interface with cloud infrastructures exposed as a service (IaaS). The Open Cloud Computing Interface (OCCI) is a RESTful Protocol and API for all kinds of cloud management tasks. OCCI was originally initiated to create a remote management API for IaaS model-based services, allowing for the development of interoperable tools for common tasks including deployment, autonomic scaling, and monitoring. It has since evolved into a flexible API with a strong focus on interoperability while still offering a

high degree of extensibility. The current release of the Open Cloud Computing Interface is suitable to serve many other models in addition to IaaS, including PaaS and SaaS.

Object Management Group (OMG)

The OMG was founded in 1989 and develops standards for enterprise integration. Its membership is international and is open to any organization, both computer industry vendors and software end users. Specific cloud-related specification efforts have only just begun in OMG, focusing on modeling deployment of applications and services on clouds for portability, interoperability, and reuse.

Storage Networking Industry Association (SNIA)

SNIA Cloud TWG
The SNIA has created the Cloud Storage Technical Work Group for the purpose of developing SNIA Architecture related to system implementations of cloud storage technology. The cloud Storage TWG:

- Acts as the primary technical entity for the SNIA to identify, develop, and coordinate systems standards for cloud storage;
- Produces a comprehensive set of specifications and drives consistency of interface standards and messages across the various cloud storage-related efforts; and
- Documents system-level requirements and shares these with other cloud storage standards organizations under the guidance of the SNIA Technical Council and in cooperation with the SNIA Strategic Alliances Committee.

SNIA Cloud Data Management Interface (CDMI)
The CDMI specification is now a SNIA Architecture standard and has been submitted to the INCITS organization for ratification as an ANSI and ISO standard as well.

SNIA Terms and Diagrams
SNIA and OGF have collaborated on cloud storage for a cloud computing white paper. A demo of this architecture has been implemented and shown several times. More information can be found at the Cloud Demo Google Group.

Trusted Computing Group (TCG)

The TCG is a not-for-profit organization formed to develop, define, and promote open, vendor-neutral industry standards for trusted computing building blocks and software interfaces across multiple platforms. TCG has approximately 100 members from across the computing industry, including component vendors, software developers, systems vendors, and network and infrastructure companies.

Telecommunications Industry Association (TIA)

The TIA is accredited by the American National Standards Institute (ANSI) as a standards developing organization (SDO). TIA has created the Cloud Computing Subcommittee (CCSC).

Acting as a liaison between TIA's twelve engineering committees, the CCSC hosts monthly calls open to TIA member companies and engineering committee participants. The focus of these calls is to address ways TIA engineering committees may develop or amend TIA standards pertaining to cloud services. The CCSC also maintains liaison relationships with national and international standards development organizations (SDOs) to determine how existing TIA standards may be adopted to avoid duplication of efforts

TM Forum

TM Forum is a global, non-profit industry association focused on enabling service provider agility and innovation. As an established thought-leader in service creation, management and delivery, the Forum serves as a unifying force across industries, enabling more than 900 member companies to solve critical business issues through access to a wealth of knowledge, intellectual capital and standards.

The Forum provides a unique, fair, and safe environment for the entire value-chain to collaborate and overcome the barriers to a vibrant, open digital economy, helping member companies of all sizes gain a competitive edge by enabling efficiency and agility in their IT and operations.

TM Forum's Digital Services Initiative focuses on overcoming the end-to-end management challenges of complex digital services, enabling an open, vibrant digital economy. The Forum's work in cloud is targeted at solving the challenges faced by members as they deliver and consume digital services hosted in the cloud.

World Wide Web Consortium (W3C)

Founded in 1994, the W3C is a non-incorporated international community of 334 Member organizations that develop standards in support of web technologies. The W3C work in the area of cyber security standards includes secure transferring data from one domain to another domain or between applications with well-defined document authentication. XML Encryption and XML Signature are key pieces of the XML security stack.

16 APPENDIX E – CONCEPTUAL MODELS AND ARCHITECTURES

General reference models:

- Distributed Management Task Force (DMTF): Cloud Service Reference Architecture
- Cloud Computing Use Case Discussion Group: a taxonomy for cloud computing
- IBM: Cloud Reference Architecture
- Cloud Security Alliance: Cloud Reference Model
- Cisco Cloud Reference Architecture Framework
- IETF: Cloud Reference Framework
- ITU-T Focus Group Cloud Reference Architecture

Reference models focusing on specific application requirements:

- Open Security Architecture: Secure Architecture Models
- GSA: FCCI (Federal Cloud Computing Initiative)
- Juniper Networks: Cloud-ready Data Center Reference Architecture
- SNIA standard: Cloud Data Management Interface
- Elastra: A Cloud Technology Reference Model for Enterprise Clouds

17 APPENDIX F – EXAMPLES OF USG CRITERIA FOR SELECTION OF STANDARDS

USG Approach to Selecting Standards

F-1 Analysis Model for Selection of Private Sector Consensus Standards[26]

NIST has developed a model set of questions to use when evaluating private sector consensus standards for agency use:

Applicability of standard

- Is it clear who should use the standard and for what applications?
- How does the standard fit into the Federal Enterprise Architecture (FEA)?
- What was done to investigate viable alternative standards (i.e., due diligence) before selecting this standard?

Availability of standard

- Is the standard published and publicly available?
- Is a copy of the standard free or must it be purchased?
- Are there any licensing requirements for using the standard?

Completeness of standard

- To what degree does the candidate standard define and cover the key features necessary to support the specific E-Gov functional area or service?

Implementations on standard

- Does the standard have strong support in the commercial marketplace?
- What commercial products exist for this standard?
- Are there products from different vendors in the market to implement this standard?
- Are there any existing or planned mechanisms to assess conformity of implementations to the standard?

---

[26] http://www.nist.gov/standardsgov/analysis-model-for-selection-of-consensus-standards.cfm

Interoperability of implementations

- How does this standard provide users the ability to access applications and services through web services?
- What are the existing or planned mechanisms to assess the interoperability of different vendor implementations?

Legal considerations

- Are there any patent assertions made to this standard?
- Are there any Intellectual Property Rights (IPR) assertions that will hinder USG distribution of the standard?

Maturity of standard

- How technically mature is the standard?
- Is the underlying technology of the standard well-understood (e.g., a reference model is well-defined, appropriate concepts of the technology are in widespread use, the technology may have been in use for many years, a formal mathematical model is defined, etc.)?
- Is the standard based upon technology that has not been well-defined and may be relatively new?

Source of standard

- What standards body developed and now maintains this standard?
- Is this standard a de jure or de facto national or international standard?
- Is there an open process for revising or amending this standard?

Stability of standard

- How long has this standard been used?
- Is the standard stable (e.g., its technical content is mature)?
- Are major revisions or amendments in progress that will affect backward compatibility with the approved standard?
- When is the estimated completion date for the next version?

F-2 Department of Defense (DoD)

The DoD IT Standards Registry (DISR) mandates the minimum set of IT standards and guidelines for the acquisition of all DoD systems that produce, use, or exchange information. The Defense Information Systems Agency (DISA) is the executive agent for the DISR. The DISR is updated three times a year.

Initial Standards Selection Criteria for Inclusion in the DISR

A number of criteria should be considered when evaluating a standard for inclusion in the DISR. Selection criteria include:

- the source of the standard;
- openness;
- technology relevance;
- maturity;
- marketplace support;
- "usefulness/utility"; and
- risk.

Criteria	Description
Source of the Standard	Recognized authority
	Cooperative stance
	Feedback
	Process
	Consensus
Openness	Ownership/IPR
	User Participation
	Vendor Participation
Technology Relevance	
Maturity	Planning Horizon
	Stability
	Revision Content & Schedule
Marketplace Support	Acceptance
	Commercial Viability
Usefulness/Utility	Well-Defined Quality Attributes
	Services & Application Interoperability
Risk	Performance, maturity & stability issues

Table 18 – DoD Selection Criteria and Description Summary

Standards Source

DoD policy articulates a preference hierarchy based on the source (owner/sponsor/publisher) of the standard. Note that the 5th Priority, Military, has its own internal priority of international first and then DoD MIL-STDs.

The standards preference hierarchy is:

Priority	Standards Source Hierarchy	Example
1st	International	ISO, IEC, ITU
2nd	National	ANSI
3rd	Professional Society; Technology Consortia; Industry Association	IEEE; IETF; W3C; OASIS; GEIA
4th	Government	FIPS
5th	Military	MIL-STDS, STANAGS

Table 19 – DoD Standards Sources Preferences

The standard must be recognized as being available from a reputable and authoritative source. The responsible SDO/Standard Setting Organization (SSO) must have an established position within the relevant technical, professional, and marketplace communities as an objective authority in its sphere of activity. This means that the standard has been created and approved/adopted/published via a formal process and configuration management of the standard has been established. Accreditation implies acceptance by a recognized authoritative SSO.

The Standards Selection Criteria also provides guidance for moving through the standards life cycle that changes the category of a standard from "emerging" to "mandated" to "inactive/retired."

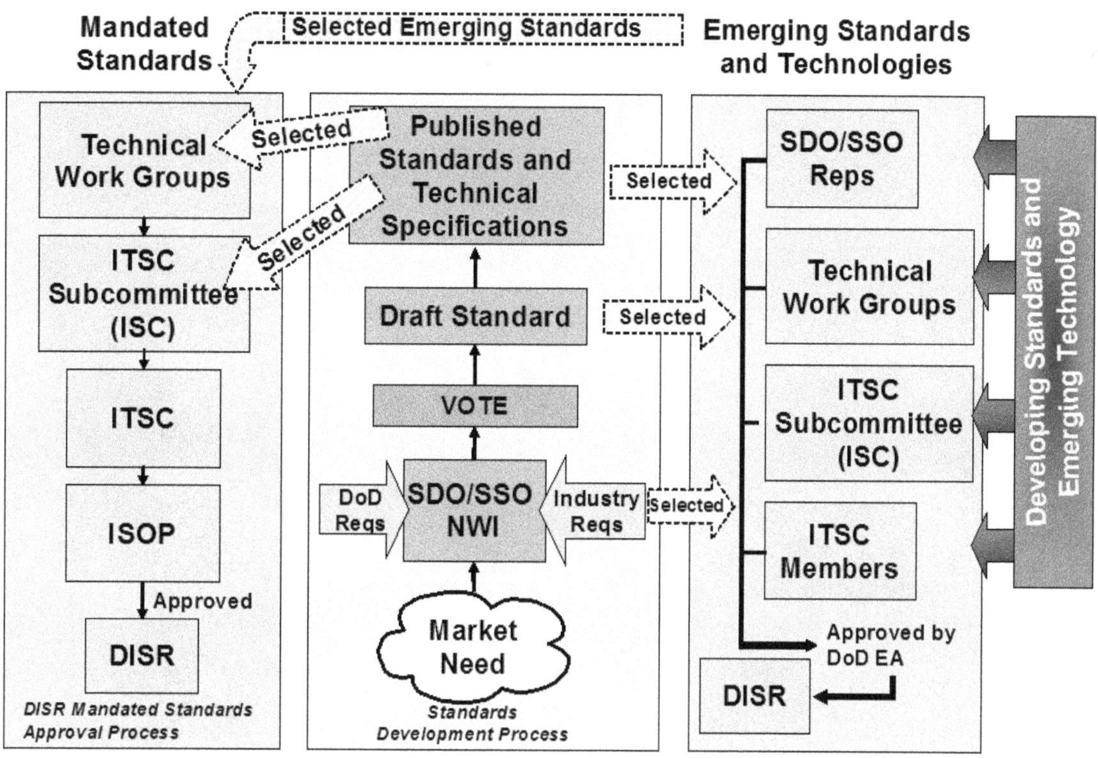

Figure 13 – DoD DISR Standards Selection Process

www.ingramcontent.com/pod-product-compliance
Lightning Source LLC
Chambersburg PA
CBHW080556060326
40689CB00021B/4872
* 9 7 8 1 4 9 4 7 9 4 4 7 7 *